FIONA AGOMBAR

Endless
ENERGY

OVER
50 WAYS TO
FIGHT FATIGUE

BCA

LONDON   NEW YORK   SYDNEY   TORONTO

This edition published 2002
by BCA
by arrangement with Piatkus
a division of Judy Piatkus (Publishers) Limited

CN 102714

Text design by Paul Saunders
Edited by Carol Franklin
Illustrations by Lesley Wakerley

Typeset by Phoenix Photosetting, Chatham, Kent
Printed and bound in Great Britain by
Mackays of Chatham plc, Chatham, Kent

Acknowledgements

I am indebted to my friends, Jo and Jackie Cary-Elwes, Sandy Webb, Elaine Myers and Angela Stevens for their invaluable comments on my first draft, Stephanie de la Warr for her 'fuel analogy' and another huge thank you to Elaine for her input with the recipes. Also thanks to Julian Campbell at Empulse, Pat Herington and John Thie at Touch for Health, Jacqui Beacon at Environmental Harmony, Stephen Walpole, Monique Edmonston, Lizzie Spring, Revd Lindsay Hammond and Dr Jack Levenson. A special thank you to Susan Fleming and Sandra Rigby, my editors, who have made such positive suggestions to make this a better book and to Dr Sarah Myhill for her help. Most of all, I want to thank my husband, Roy, for his support and technical wizardry with my computer.

Contents

PART III **Food and Energy**

PART IV **Exercise and Therapies for Energy**

PART V **Energise Your Environment**

PART VI **The Mind-Body-Spirit Solution to your Energy Crisis**

READ THIS BEFORE YOU START...

Tired. Drained. Exhausted. No spark. Wrung out. Just about getting through each day. Does this describe you? Then this book could change your life, as it will tell you how to have more energy than you thought possible, by making only a few very simple adjustments to your life. The book is divided into short, easily-digested chapters, so you can dip in as you wish.

This book is based on what I learned through experience of devastating fatigue following a chronic illness. In 1990, after prolonged stress caused by running my own business, I caught glandular fever. I became very ill, and my fatigue was so overwhelming that even holding a five-minute conversation would exhaust me. Eventually I spent six months in a wheelchair, diagnosed with Chronic Fatigue Syndrome (ME). At the time, I was desperate for advice. What would help? Vitamins? Homeopathy? Reflexology? What would give me an instant increase of energy? There was a bewildering amount of information and I just didn't know where to start. This is the book I was looking for then, to help guide me out of my crippling exhaustion. Luckily for the majority of you reading this, your fatigue will not be as profound as mine was then. The point is, that there are a lot of things you can do to improve your energy levels, whatever the cause, which will give you a much needed energy boost, however severe your exhaustion.

I now teach yoga, but I'm not just another health practitioner dishing out academic advice that is difficult to follow. What makes this book different is that I am writing from my own experience; I know what works, because I have been there. There are some 50 ideas in here to help you energise and revitalise. What they all have in common is that they are simple to do, and they are all based on common sense. Some can give you an instant lift, and some will make you think and perhaps point you in a new, healthier direction. Some of the advice is repeated throughout the book, but I don't apologise for this, as there are important points that need to be emphasised if you really want to beat fatigue for ever.

What I have learned is that increasing your energy is not about trying a pick-and-mix method of various remedies. Nor is there a magic pill or bullet that will stop your tiredness. Beating fatigue is about looking at your body and energy system as a whole. So, yes, of course you can go to a shop and get instant (but temporary) energy in a bar or even a jar. But, really, your energy levels are a barometer of your overall health. And if you are tired all the time, then you need to stop right now and think about your life – what you do, what you eat, what exercise you do or don't take – and reappraise it. Tiredness is your early-warning system; telling you to look after yourself. And this is where I hope this book will help you to change your life by getting to the root cause of what is making you tired, so that you can do something about it.

Tiredness, or fatigue, incidentally, is the most common reason for people in the Western world to visit their doctors. A recent survey in the US found that tiredness was a serious problem for nearly a quarter of the population. So if you are exhausted or stressed, you are not alone. But please, if you are tired all the time, do get your health checked out first by your own doctor before you read this book, just to be sure that there is no serious underlying cause for your fatigue. Even if there is, some of the ideas in this book will still be able to help you.

The book is divided into six parts. I begin by looking at stress and effective ways of dealing with it, as this so often underlies fatigue problems. Part II looks at possible physical problems that could be causing your fatigue and effective self-help treatments. For example, food intolerances and chemical sensitivities can often cause tiredness but can be overcome with some simple lifestyle changes. Part III looks at the key area to increase energy – nutrition – and gives you some simple ideas to immediately put into practice, from drinking more water, to which herbs to take for more energy. Part IV looks at exercise and therapies for energy, from yoga to aromatherapy. Part V gives you tips for making your home and work environment healthy and energising, while Part VI shows you how to ensure your mind, body and spirit are all working harmoniously to enhance your vitality.

Finally, in yoga, it is believed that energy is all around us. It is just a matter of knowing how to tap into it. And this is exactly what this book will help *you* to do. Good luck.

Fiona Agombar

PART I

Stress And How To Beat It

Stress is one of the major contributing causes of tiredness and many of us suffer from stress without even knowing it. Many people discount the long-term effect of emotional strain – both major and minor life events can have a dramatic effect on your energy levels. From moving home to starting a new job, or from relationship problems to frustration at work, stress may be sapping your energy to a surprising degree. Part I shows first how stress can affect you both mentally and physically, then how you can boost your stamina with some very simple steps to reduce tension.

1

How Stress Can Affect You

Did you know that stress is the most common cause of fatigue? And did you know that you might be suffering from stress without even realising it? This might sound incredible, but it's true. What happens when you are under pressure is that your body slowly adapts to it, but at the cost of all kinds of physical and mental side-effects. Some of the warning signs to look out for include high blood pressure, rapid breathing, poor sleep, sweating, feeling 'spacey', panic attacks, feeling low, depressed and irritable, *and exhaustion.*

Generally, stress occurs when you are faced with events that you may see as threatening to your physical or mental well-being. These events are referred to as stressors, and your reactions to them are your stress responses. Countless events create stress. Major changes in your life such as the death of a close relative, illness, divorce or change of job, for instance, would cause most people stress. However, in this age of technology with our busier lifestyles, many more people feel under constant pressure and can be said to be leading continually stressful lives.

THE FIGHT OR FLIGHT RESPONSE

Research has shown that the more uncontrollable your life or a particular event seems to you, the more likely it will be perceived by you as stressful. The key word here is *perception*. For example, an event that you may find stressful, someone else may find stimulating or challenging.

When you are under stress, a number of physiological changes happen in your body that trigger something known as the 'fight or flight' response. This is the same bodily reaction that helped our ancestors to survive by making them fit for dealing with or fleeing from dangerous, life-threatening situations. In the old days, we had to cope with hunting wild animals or escaping from predators, and a stress response in the body was triggered; what is known as the autonomic system cut in. Your body gears itself up to deal with stress in the same way today. These reactions are largely unconscious: in other words, *you may not be aware of them* as they happen. In your brain the hypothalamus gland sends electrical and chemical messages to the pituitary gland, which is responsible for hormone production. A hormone called ACTH is then sent to your adrenal glands, which release over 30 chemicals, including cortisol and adrenalin. These hormones release sugar from your liver, make your heart beat faster, your muscles tense, your breathing more rapid, your digestion slow down and your blood pressure rise. All this is done to give you a rapid increase in energy so that you can physically face up to or flee from difficult situations.

However, this response is usually inappropriate for coping with the stresses of life in the twenty-first century.

For example, if you are trying to cope with work, children, the house and a busy social life, you may perceive these as stressors, and you will consequently have the same response that our ancestors had – and woosh – off your autonomic system goes! So, if you have tension at work or at home, you will get the same symptoms as our ancestors did when trying to get out of trouble. This is OK, if it doesn't happen too often, as your body just switches itself back to normal after the problem has passed. However, if you live or work in an environment where you are under constant pressure, you may *adapt* to stress. In other words, you will find you are continually switched into this fight or flight response.

HOW DO YOU KNOW IF YOU ARE SUFFERING FROM STRESS?

If you have adapted to stress, you may notice that you feel below par and are tired all the time, as if you are not functioning on all cylinders. This is because your autonomic nervous system has got used to the fight or flight response and cannot switch your body back to normal. This is very tiring, as you are constantly using energy to keep your body wound up in this response to stress. At this point, you may start to use stimulants such as coffee, cigarettes, alcohol or sugar to give you an extra boost of energy. This is, in fact, the *worst* thing you can do, as, although you will feel a temporary surge of energy, this will put a further strain on your system. It's a bit like whipping a horse that has already run a race. There is no real energy left in your weakened system, which really needs rest and relaxation at this crucial time.

I know this from experience, because I never listened to my own body until it was too late. I ran a busy public relations consultancy in the 1980s and worked long hours without rest or relaxation. Eventually, the continual pressure I was suffering from caused me to become ill. I wish that I had understood the symptoms of stress then and taken the appropriate action to deal with it.

If you are not listening to your own symptoms of stress and fatigue, you may also eventually become ill. For example, you may suffer from high blood pressure, low blood sugar, rapid breathing and a feeling of anxiety *most of the time.* These symptoms can lead to further health problems associated with fatigue (as you will see when you read Chapter 6 on breathing and Chapter 21 on blood sugar). But the root cause is stress and here are some of the signs to look for:

- Feeling tired and exhausted, but also over-stimulated, as if you have drunk too much caffeine

- Feeling anxious

- Suffering from irritability or anger and losing your sense of humour

- Finding it difficult to concentrate

- Not sleeping well

- Finding that you are more vulnerable to infections like colds and flu

- High blood pressure

- Apathy and depression

You may have some of these symptoms – or all of them. As I have already mentioned, you may not even be aware of these symptoms until you really think about it.

Tips To Banish Stress

Here are some very simple techniques that you can use to make your life more manageable and help revitalise your system:

- First, examine your life. Listen to your body. Remember, stress is very much to do with *perception*. In other words, it's how you see a situation. You may find your life impossibly difficult, whereas another person with the same load would cope or even find it a challenge. Take note of what is making you feel stressed and see if there is any way of altering the circumstances, which may help you to perceive things differently. You may be able to negotiate more time on a deadline, for example, or you may find that cutting out more social commitments from your diary will help. (You will find more advice on taking time out in Chapter 2.)

- Remember, the more out of control a situation seems to you, the more stressed you will be. Get back in control by defining your problem and looking at alternative solutions. Maybe you are setting your standards too high and need to change your level of aspiration. Being a perfectionist or a workaholic could be damaging your health. Reduce your targets: for example, if you work and have a family too, you can't keep your house looking immaculate. Your health and energy are more important than a bit of dust. By lowering your expectations of yourself, you are reducing your levels of stress.

- Slow down. Don't do one thing after another: take short breaks between tasks. And don't try to focus on more than one task at a time, otherwise you may feel overwhelmed.

- Are you breathing too fast? Slow down your breathing. Practise the breathing techniques shown in Chapter 6 until you have trained your body to breathe more slowly – *automatically*.

- Eat a good diet. Junk food actually puts more strain on your body, especially your adrenal glands. If you eat healthy food with the correct nutrients for the 'fight or flight' response it will support you in times of stress. Don't exhaust your adrenal glands with poor-quality food or stimulants (anything containing caffeine).

- Give up smoking. You will never successfully reduce your stress levels while you continue to smoke. Inhaling cigarette tobacco actually *increases* stress as it stimulates your adrenal glands. If you smoke, you are also taking over a hundred toxic chemicals into your bloodstream, and some of these reduce your oxygen supply, which directly affects your energy levels.

- Exercise helps to burn up stress. The fight or flight response was designed to help our ancestors run fast, so it makes sense that if you take regular exercise, you are using all those stress hormones that would otherwise be just swimming around in your system.

- Seek emotional support from close friends or family. Talking a problem through can reduce your levels of stress significantly, as can writing your problems down in a diary.

- Take up activities and hobbies. Temporarily setting aside thinking about your problems is very helpful. Going to the cinema, reading a good book or magazine, playing with children or taking some exercise will give you a breather from your negative feelings and can help put you in control again. (However, remember that this is not the same as avoiding the issue by using drink or drugs which will only make things worse in the long run.)

- Finally, relaxation, relaxation, relaxation. Numerous studies have shown that the most important way to tackle stress and re-energise is by learning how to relax. Practise the relaxation exercise given on page 15, every day. Learn to tell the difference between tense and relaxed muscles, so next time you are in a situation that makes you tense, you can relax your muscles.

Remember, it is appropriate to have the stress reaction if you are being chased by a wild animal, but not if you are having an argument with your partner! So take back control, look at what you can change and start to reduce any stress that you have in your life.

2

Beat Stress and Fatigue – Learn to Take Time Out

There could be a very simple reason for your stress and fatigue. In fact, the reason is so obvious, it is something that most of us just don't think about. *You may be tired because you are doing too much!* Being too busy is a common stressor of the twenty-first century. Perhaps you know this already, but you think you can't stop – you have to keep cramming gallons of activities into a pint-sized time schedule. And, yes, some people do seem to be able to do loads of things without getting tired. However, you probably aren't one of these super-human types, which is why you are reading this book!

GETTING BALANCE IN YOUR LIFE

Life has to be balanced. You have to put back in as much as you take out. So, if you spend a lot of your time rushing around, working, looking after your children, looking after your house, trying to keep up with a busy social life, and so on, remember that you also need to make time for rest and relaxation. Holidays, short breaks and daily time out for yourself are just as important as working hard. Look at your lifestyle and start prioritising. Scrutinise your daily timetable and decide which activities are really essential, and which you can cut out to give you a better quality of life. Schedule 'me time' breaks into your diary. Ask yourself the following questions:

- Do I need such a busy social life? Isn't it better to concentrate on a few quality close friends?

- Am I trying to do too many things for other people? Am I making enough time for myself?

- What activities could I cut out of my weekly routine to give myself more time, which would, in turn, release more energy? Just asking the question 'Am I doing too much?' may show you the obvious route of your tiredness.

Tips For Taking Time Out

- Remember, you *deserve* some time off. Business schools now teach that individuals are more productive if they work shorter hours with more breaks, and if they make time for proper holidays. Apply this lesson to your own life.

- If you can, book plenty of time out. Frequent weekend breaks from everyday routine can be as beneficial as a two-week holiday. If you can't afford this, just changing your daily routine and going to stay with friends or family can be helpful.

- If you are very busy, try cooking meals ahead and freezing them. In Part III on diet you will see that freshly prepared organic food will give you more energy. However, it is important to eat proper meals at least three times a day, so if occasionally taking something out of the freezer helps you to manage your time better, do it. It's certainly much better than trying to survive on unhealthy, sugary snacks because you've run out of time and are too tired to prepare a proper meal. Another option is to eat out occasionally.

- Don't be afraid to ask for help. If you and your partner both work, then make sure that you share the cooking and cleaning tasks. If you have children, ask them to help with the dishes, and make their beds or clean their own rooms. The best piece of advice I've heard came from Dr Sarah Myhill, Medical Adviser for Action for ME. She says that we should all give up ironing as it wastes lots of energy and often isn't essential. That doesn't mean you have to be completely untidy, but it's a good idea to think about reducing unnecessary household chores.

- Don't take on too much. Learn to be assertive and say 'no' if people ask you to do too much. Think very carefully about your boundaries. People will respect you, not resent you, if you say you can't do something.

- If you are struggling with the pressures of work, prioritise each task. Divide your work into four categories: 1 Important and urgent; 2 Important but not urgent; 3 Urgent but not important; 4 Not urgent and not important. Work through these chronologically each day and *only focus on the first category*, rather than taking on tasks that you would prefer to do first. Recategorise your list every day; you will find that this will immediately take the stress and anxiety out of your daily workload.

- Fit the principle of short breaks into each day. If you can, every hour, take five minutes out just to sit quietly and relax. Make sure that you always have a proper lunch hour. And pace yourself. Don't keep your foot on the accelerator pedal of life all the time. After a period of frenetic activity, take a short break away from what you are doing. Go for a five-minute walk, for example. Balance activity with rest and relaxation every day. That way you are investing in your health and will avoid burn-out.

So, if you feel that your batteries are drained and that you need more energy, don't underestimate the value of revising your life. Taking time out from your home and work place can introduce more rest and relaxation into your life.

3

Recharge Your Batteries and Relax Your Body

It is clear that stress, anxiety and just doing too much can make you feel very tired. If you practise the following simple relaxation exercise every day, you will be amazed at how much it will replenish and revitalise you. Eventually, you will learn the difference between a tight muscle and a relaxed one. This means that if you carry this awareness with you during the day, you can consciously relax whenever you are in a stressful situation, so that you are not depleting your batteries by holding your muscles in constant tension. This will save you lots of energy, as it takes up lots of effort when your muscles are tense all the time!

It might help to get a friend to read this exercise very slowly aloud to you, or record it on to a tape, so that you don't have to keep referring to the book.

PREPARE TO RELAX

Find a quiet, warm place where you won't be disturbed. Unplug the phone and close the curtains. Tell yourself that this is your time and that you don't have to worry about anything for the next ten minutes. Try to focus your mind on the exercise. If your mind starts to wander, then gently bring it back to the here and now.

Lie down on a bed or on the floor. Make yourself comfortable with a pillow under your head, and under your knees if you like. Cover yourself with something warm, because when you relax, your blood pressure and body temperature drop. Check that your back has full contact with the floor or bed so that it can fully relax. If there is a gap under the small of your back, fold a towel and put it underneath.

THE RELAXATION EXERCISE

To start, have your legs and arms slightly spread away from your body. Just concentrate on the rhythm of your breathing. Try to slow down your breathing. Notice the difference between your in-breath and your out-breath.

Now, take your attention to your feet. Hold them about 5 cm (2 in) above the floor for a few seconds, then relax them back on to the floor. Consciously say the word 'relax' in your mind. Next, lift your legs about 5 cm (2 in) from the floor. Focus on the tension in your legs, then let them flop on to the floor, turning your feet slightly outwards. Notice the difference between how your legs felt when they were tight and how they feel when they are relaxed.

Now, make fists with your hands. Really clench your fists, then release, so that your hands are facing up to the ceiling. Next lift your arms from the floor for a few seconds, then let them fall on to the floor. Feel them growing heavy.

Take your shoulders up towards your ears, then let them drop, so that the space between your ears and shoulders increases. Now focus on your neck. Release it by turning your head from side to side.

Next, think about your navel area. Relax by visualising a warm yellow light, relaxing and releasing tension all around your solar plexus. Release your back. You should have full contact with the floor or bed – if not, adjust the towel under your back. Bend your knees if this helps you.

Check your jaw. Is it clenched? Release it, feeling the space widen between your upper and lower teeth. Now imagine that hands are massaging between your eyebrows and the back of your head. Just feel yourself growing heavier and heavier, melting into the floor. Check particular areas of tension such as your shoulders, back and jaw, then just focus on your breathing, saying the word 'Re' on your in-breath and 'lax' on your out-breath.

Continue this for a few minutes, then when you are ready, open your eyes and start to move your body gently. Roll to your left-hand side for a minute or two, then slowly get up.

If you do this exercise regularly you will begin to see that having more energy is about relaxing properly and doing less – not more.

4

Relax Your Mind

Does your brain sometimes feel as if it is always on the go, jumping from one thing to another, to another? This is a very common problem especially as so many of us are trying to do so much and suffering from information overload. In yoga, the mind is often referred to as a 'chattering monkey', and one of the main aims of yoga is to calm the mind. Muscle relaxation exercises can help to a certain extent, but the exercise given here is a really effective way of slowing down the brain. It is based on a combination of two exercises: autogenics, which encourages a deep state of mental relaxation; and yoga nidra, which uses the concentration technique of focusing on parts of the body, by slowly moving your attention from one part to another. Focusing and concentration are very effective ways of learning to still the mind, and have a similar effect to self-hypnosis. If you practise this exercise regularly, you will notice a big increase in your energy. Indeed, this exercise can be as calming and refreshing as a period of deep sleep.

You can learn the exercise and train yourself to go round your body, focusing slowly on each part. Even better is to read this on to tape, or to get a friend to read it to you *slowly* as you practise.

EXERCISE FOR CALMING THE MIND

First, choose a place where you won't be disturbed. Lie quietly on your back, on the floor or on a bed. Try to relax your body as much as possible. Make yourself really comfortable. Tell yourself that you are not going to sleep, but that you are going to focus on each part of your body in turn. As you focus, really feel the part you are concentrating on and try to relax that part even further. If your mind wanders, don't worry, just gently bring it back and concentrate. Take three long, deep and slow breaths. On each out-breath, tell yourself to relax, letting go of tension.

Now, become aware of any sounds that you can hear in the room. Next, notice any sounds you can hear outside the building. Don't analyse the sounds, just be aware of them.

Bring your attention back to your body. Notice where your body is touching the floor or the bed. Your ankles, your calves and thighs, head, top of your back, your hips, your arms and hands – just observe where you are making contact. Next, notice the spaces between you and your support. Just go round your body and be aware where there are any gaps.

You are now going to take your attention to each part of your body in turn. Start with the right thumb, index finger, middle finger, ring finger, little finger, right palm. Feel the whole of your right hand. Back of your right hand, wrist, lower arm, elbow, upper arm, shoulder, armpit, right side of your body, right waist, hip, back of the right leg, right thigh, right knee, right calf muscle, ankle, heel, sole, top of your right foot, right big toe, second toe, third toe, fourth, toe, little toe. Repeat the process for your left side, starting with your left thumb.

If your mind has drifted off, bring it back. Go to the top of your head, forehead, right eyebrow, left eyebrow, the space between your eyebrows, right eyelid, left eyelid, right eye, left eye, right cheek, left cheek, right ear, left ear, upper lip, lower lip, chin, jaw, throat, right collarbone, left collarbone, your chest, your navel, your groin, whole of your right leg, whole of your left leg.

Now move your attention to your back. Feel the whole of your back. Next, feel your whole body becoming heavy. Notice your left leg feeling heavy and warm. Now your right leg is getting heavy and warm. Notice your right arm growing heavy and warm. Your left arm is getting heavy and warm. Your head is growing heavy and warm. Your whole body is getting very warm, as if you are lying in hot sunshine. Become aware again of where your body is making contact with the floor.

Now imagine that you are lying in the sun and you are getting very warm. Visualise your whole body lying on a beautiful beach. Feel the warmth. As you breathe in, you are breathing in energy. As you breathe out, you are breathing out any tension. Follow your breath, breathing in energy and breathing out tension. Now feel your whole body becoming lighter. Your left leg, your right leg, your left arm, your right arm. Your head. Your whole body is so light you feel that you could float away.

Now start to become aware of your body, where it is lying, and the room. Start to bring yourself back to the here and now. Rub your palms vigorously together. Cup them over your eyes. Count to five, open your eyes, remove your hands and have a big stretch.

5

Sleeping Deep Sleep

Sleep is the best antidote to stress that there is. However, if you are suffering from stress then it is very likely that you are not sleeping so well. Your quality of sleep will, of course, contribute significantly to your energy. Ask yourself how you sleep. Do you fall asleep quickly, sleeping for up to eight hours, then wake up feeling refreshed? Or do you find it difficult to nod off every night and wake up early with your mind racing?

Upto 90 per cent of people suffer from insomnia at some time. However, most people who think that they have not slept all night will usually have managed at least three or four hours. The question to ask is how much sleeplessness is affecting your quality of life and your energy levels. Worrying about the number of hours that you get will only cause you more sleep disturbance.

Insomnia generally falls into three types: sleeplessness that lasts just a few days; short term, which may last up to three weeks; and chronic, which is long term. The majority of these problems then falls into one of two categories: either difficulty in getting to sleep; or problems with staying asleep. In the first situation, stress, worry, caffeine, alcohol, change of surroundings and worries about losing sleep are common causes. In the latter, if you wake up after only a few hours of sleep then it may be linked to an underlying psychological problem such as anxiety or depression. Sleep deprivation, will of course, make things worse. Lack of sleep will make you even more irritable, stressed, anxious and depressed, as well as weakening your immunity to viral infections and reducing your ability to cope with things the next day.

The question of how much sleep you need is very much down to the individual. Some people can survive on five hours a night, whereas others feel terrible unless they have had at least nine hours. About 90 per cent of adults sleep from six to nine hours per night, with the largest number needing between seven-and-a-half to eight hours to be free of daytime sleepiness.

You And Your Brain Waves

Everything you do is affected by the brain, which is made up of chemical and electromagnetic digital signals, created by billions of nerve endings sending pulsed messages from around your body, back to your brain.

Your brain produces electrical signals in a range between 0.5–120 waves or Hertz (a measurement of times per second). These are split into: Delta 0.5–3 Hertz (lower, slower waves that occur during deep sleep); Theta 4–7 Hertz (higher wave bands that relate to artistic, creative and intellectual thought process, and also to rapid eye movement, or light sleep); Alpha 8–12 Hertz (conscious, physical relaxation and the first stage of sleep); and Beta 13–15

Hertz (conscious thinking when awake, sensory input, automatic processes and emotional states). There are also Gamma brain waves, which are higher, but not much is understood about these.

Anything can affect these brain waves, from drinking coffee, through to exposure to electromagnetic fields such as mobile phones or radio alarm clocks. Understanding your brain waves and how they are affected by stress, may help you to enjoy a better quality of sleep.

The stages of sleep

Analysis of the pattern of brain waves shows that sleep involves five stages. The first four are known as non-rapid eye movement (NREM) and stage five as rapid eye movement (REM). When you are awake, your brain waves are spiky and irregular and are associated with the Beta range. When you close your eyes and relax, your brain waves start to slow into a regular pattern of 8 to 12 Hertz, or Alpha waves. At this point you start to drift into stage one sleep. In stage two, your brain will show short runs of rhythmical responses. As you fall deeper into stages three and four, your brain produces even slower Delta waves (1 to 2 Hertz). At this point your eye movements are virtually absent, your heart and breathing rate decrease, and there is increased muscle relaxation. Generally, you will be hard to arouse during stages three and four of sleep.

After you have been asleep for an hour or so, your brain becomes very active and, even though you are asleep, your eyes will move rapidly under your eyelids. This is stage five or REM sleep. During REM sleep, your eye movements occur in bursts lasting 10 to 20 seconds, your heart rate increases, as does your brain's metabolic rate. This is the sleeping period in which you are more likely to experience vivid, unusual or illogical dreams. These various stages of sleep alternate throughout the night and research has shown that we need to experience all the stages of sleep during the night, in order to wake refreshed.

Your internal clock

Your body functions on the circadian rhythm which is a natural period of approximately 25 hours. This is your own internal clock and affects your temperature, metabolism and, of course, sleep. Your circadian clock takes cues from the environment, such as light and dark, which you need to keep you synchronised with the outside world. In the old days, when candlelight was all there was, people tended to keep to the natural rhythms of the earth – going to sleep when it was dark and waking up when it was light. People also slept longer in the winter months.

Anything that upsets your daily clock, such as light, stress or activity, which trigger your 'awake' hormones, can affect your sleep. Your body produces various hormones and chemicals as this internal clock runs; for example, you produce corticosteroids, which work with adrenalin early in the morning, to tell your body it is time to get up. Light will also help to trigger some of your 'awake' hormones, which usually peak at around midday. At night, as it becomes dark, your brain produces melatonin, which makes you feel sleepy. There is some evidence that production of melatonin falls with increasing age. In the US, melatonin can be bought over the counter (but not in the UK) and is often used to help reset the body clock to help with jet lag. Growth hormone is also produced at night during sleep, especially during NREM sleep. This means that the blood supply to your body increases, tissue grows and repairs, and your immune system is boosted. In other words, much of your body's repair happens while you are sleeping.

If your hormones get out of kilter, so that you are producing daytime hormones during the night and vice versa, then you are going to have sleep problems. This is a sign that your circadian rhythm has been disrupted and understanding how this works may be the key for you to know how to reset your body's clock so that you can sleep better. Ideally, you should have the least adrenalin during the night, and the least growth hormone during the day. People who work night shifts commonly suffer insomnia as their body clock is not allowed to run normally. Parents whose sleep is frequently disturbed by a wakeful child may end up suffering from chronic insomnia, because the constant interruptions disturb the body's natural rhythm. This is why it is important to have a dark room and a regular time that you go to bed and get up in the morning when it is light. It is also vital that you don't do anything too stimulating before you go to sleep. For example, watching television or reading a very exciting book may raise your adrenalin levels, which will prevent you from sleeping.

Tips For Beating Insomnia

- Probably the most important step you can take in promoting your body's natural rhythm is to get up at the same time every morning, even at weekends. Your body needs a routine and this is the way you can start to train your internal, circadian clock so that you fall asleep at the same time every night.

- If you have the odd bad night, don't lie awake worrying about it. Tell yourself that it doesn't matter. If the problem continues, however, follow the advice given in Part I to help you to tackle any stress in your life. As a last resort, you could consider seeing your doctor for a short course of sleeping tablets, to get your body back into its routine. However you should be aware that sleeping tablets can lead to fragmented sleep and can be addictive.

- If you are worried about something, get up and write down your thoughts. The problem is less likely to whizz around your head then. Consider counselling if the problem is very bad.

- Keep your bedroom at the right temperature (around 16–19° C or 60–66° F). If you are too hot or cold, then you won't sleep.

- Some insomniacs have beaten their problem with a hot water bottle and socks! This can help your body to adjust to the right temperature.

- A warm (not hot) bath can help you to become calm and gets your body at the right temperature for sleeping. Add a handful of bath salts or aromatherapy oils, such as lavender, which promotes relaxation, and light some candles. Soak for at least 15 minutes. Prepare yourself for bed in this way every night so that your body clock can adjust to this pattern of winding down for sleep.

- Make sure that your bedroom, bedding and bed clothes are comfortable.

- Avoid heavy food, strenuous exercise or alcohol for at least four hours before you go to bed. All interfere with sleep. However, a fall in your blood sugar levels can cause you to wake up, so a light snack, two hours before your bed time, may help. (People on a diet often suffer from insomnia.)

- Don't smoke! Smoking is very stimulating to the adrenal system. Avoid caffeine after 4pm. Instead, a cup of camomile tea (well known for its relaxing properties) can help you to fall asleep.

- Use your bedroom for sleeping, not for watching TV or working.

- Make sure you don't have any transformers (i.e. copper coils found in electric wall plugs) near your head. The electromagnetic radiation may interfere with your quality of sleep. (For more on this, see Chapter 36.)

- A warm, milky drink and a banana contain amino acids that may help you to fall asleep. You could also try taking a calcium and magnesium tablet at night, as these help to relax your muscles.

- Play a relaxation tape, on a walkman if you don't sleep alone, to help you to drift off to sleep.

- Gentle exercise taken every day will help you to sleep better. Vigorous exercise in the evening, however, will keep you awake.

- Natural remedies such as valerian, wild lettuce extract, passiflora and hops, available at most health-food shops, may help.

- If you sleep with a snorer, consider separate bedrooms. Otherwise buy ear plugs.

- Because light triggers off your daytime hormones make sure that your room is dark enough. If you need to get up in the night, try not to turn the light on, as this will cue your body's clock into wakefulness. You may find that an eye mask helps. Conversely, when you want to wake up and energise, let in the light to get your system going – open the curtains and stand by the window.

If you do have insomnia, one of the best steps you can take is to do the relaxation exercise given on page 15 every night. This will help prepare you for sleep, as relaxation helps the brain to produce Alpha waves, associated with the first stage of sleep.

6

Breathing for Energy

A very common cause of fatigue is over-breathing or hyper-ventilation. This means that you may be breathing too fast, only using your upper chest area as you inhale and exhale. This really is the quickest way to exhaustion. Over-breathing is often caused by stress. You will remember that the fight or flight system triggers off shallow, faster breathing. The problem is, if you adapt to stress, you learn to breathe too fast *all of the time*. It may seem strange that breathing can have such a profound effect on our vitality. The incredible thing is that many people in the Western world hyperventilate without realising it. So, slow your breathing down and dramatically improve your energy!

OXYGEN OR CARBON DIOXIDE?

When you breathe in, you absorb oxygen, which is essential to maintain all of your systems through the correct aeration of your blood. Oxygen penetrates your lung tissues to dissolve in your blood and is pumped with other nutrients through tiny capillaries to nourish everything in the body.

When you breathe out you get rid of waste gases such as carbon dioxide.

You may now think that you need more oxygen for energy. Well, actually what you need is a balance of oxygen *and* carbon dioxide. If you breathe too fast you breathe off *too much* carbon dioxide, which, in turn, will make your whole system too alkaline. A certain amount of carbon dioxide is needed to help your cells maintain the correct level of acidity. Also, oxygen is only readily released from your cells in the presence of the right levels of carbon dioxide.

Many people have the sensation that they are not getting enough oxygen to their lungs. The response to this is to breathe more deeply and faster. All that then happens is that, as carbon dioxide is breathed off, the oxygen delivery to the cells in your body is more inefficient. So, to improve oxygen delivery, you actually need to breathe less!

How Do You Know If You Are Breathing Too Fast?

If you breathe off too much carbon dioxide this can lead to lots of health problems, including a feeling of being unreal or spaced out, panic attacks, insomnia, vivid dreams, numbness in your hands and lips, muscle twitching and aches, yawning a lot or wanting to take a deep breath, dizziness or faintness – and profound fatigue.

You will notice that in different situations your breathing rate will change. For example, if you are concentrating, your breathing will slow down or even stop for a few seconds as you are holding your breath. If you are under extreme stress, this will induce rapid breathing. (Remember, for the fight or flight system, you would need to breathe fast if you were fleeing from a dangerous situation.) However, if you are continually under stress and are breathing much too fast, this may trigger a panic attack because of the physiological effect that breathing off too much carbon dioxide has on your body. If this happens, breathe slowly into a paper bag, or into your cupped hands, so that you take the exhaled carbon dioxide back into your system.

FINDING YOUR DIAPHRAGM

Your diaphragm is a large, sheet-type muscle, connected to your ribs which, if used properly, acts as a piston, filling your lungs with air and massaging your internal organs. If you use your diaphragm effectively and, if you breathe slowly, there is a better exchange of oxygen and carbon dioxide in your system. If you only breathe from your upper chest area, then you are not using your diaphragm as it is meant to be used. To find your diaphragm, place one hand on your upper chest and the other on your rib-cage. The hand on your upper chest shouldn't move too much, whereas the hand on your rib-cage should move much more noticeably as you breathe. If this is not the case, you are not breathing properly.

Tips For Breathing For Energy

The following tips will help you to learn to breathe properly and will really increase your energy levels.

- Remember, your breathing is largely driven by your unconscious, but you can override it and learn to breathe properly. If you are breathing more than 18 times a minute, you are probably breathing too fast.

- Always breathe through your nose. This will stop you from taking in great gulps of air.

- Try this easy exercise for ten minutes every day. Lie on the floor or on your bed and identify your diaphragm area around the rib-cage. One in-breath and one out-breath are one cycle. Now, try to slow your breathing down to eight to ten cycles per minute, without breathing from your upper chest area. Don't take in huge gulps of air. Aim to breathe slowly and smoothly.

- Check yourself several times a day. Are you still breathing from your diaphragm? Can you slow your breathing down?

And finally, remember: regular, slow breaths give you the most benefit. Shallow breathing gives you the least, so you should try to aim for around ten breaths every minute to maximise the physical benefits to your system. By becoming aware of your breathing rate, you will then be able to train yourself to regulate it. The more you slow your breathing down when you are stressed, the calmer you will feel, and the more energy you will have.

7

Check Your Posture

Stress can have a devastating effect on your posture and bad posture in turn, will cause you to become more tired. When you are under pressure, your back and neck muscles tense, your shoulders lift and you may stoop or hunch forward. How are you sitting now? How do you stand? Are you actually *aware* of your posture? If you slump, this will add to your fatigue, as you are restricting the major organs of your body, as well as fluids in your spine and cranium, which need to flow properly for maximum energy. However, probably the most profound effect that poor posture has is on your breathing. If you are slightly squashed forward, then your diaphragm will be restricted. If your diaphragm can't work properly, then you will end up feeling very fatigued and out of balance. In summary, poor posture restricts blood flow so that eventually there is less oxygen reaching your cells. And that means much less energy for you!

CEREBROSPINAL FLUID

Your spine contains unique fluids that take oxygen and nutrients to your head and also draw any waste or toxins away from your brain. The cerebrospinal fluid has its own rhythm that pulses at about 10 to 14 cycles per second. This fluid is vital for the health of every cell in your body and also affects your internal respiration; in other words, how you convert oxygen into energy. When your cerebrospinal fluid is flowing as it should be, your energy levels will be enhanced. However, many things can interfere with this pulse, including stress and poor posture. So, remember, if you stoop or hunch, you are interfering with this fluid and you will feel more tired. If you have good posture however, you will feel less tired as your cerebrospinal fluid will be able to flow as it should.

The spine of a baby in the womb is held in a single, protected curve. When the baby is born, there is no muscle in the neck to hold the head upright. The child slowly develops neck muscles over a period of about six to eight months. As the neck muscle gets stronger, the child starts to crawl. If you watch young children, you will notice that they will generally start with same-side crawling (left hand and left leg) and then develop into the cross-crawl (right leg and left arm). This is all done for a purpose, as the cross-crawl continually challenges both hemispheres of the brain, helping the child to balance and to concentrate. It also helps to develop muscles in the back and the buttocks and thereby prepares the body for standing. As adults, we can make use of the cross-crawl method whenever we want to re-energise.

THE CROSS-CRAWL EXERCISE

This is a very simple exercise you can do any time you feel tired. Although you may find this a little bizarre at first, it is an excellent exercise that really works. Simply get down on all fours on the floor and crawl around for five minutes, using the cross-crawl method of crawling using opposite limbs. This is a very energising exercise because it helps to reprogramme the motor cortex in the brain and will help you to concentrate and co-ordinate better. It will also clear a foggy head and helps to stimulate the cerebrospinal fluid, which will help to revitalise every cell in your body.

Sitting for long periods at a desk, particularly if you are working at a computer, can be very tiring and puts stress on your physical body. Ideally, you should work for no more than 20 minutes, without getting up to walk around or do the cross-crawl. However, this isn't always practicable, so, here are some remedial actions you can take to make sure that your posture isn't suffering too badly, causing you to become fatigued.

Tips For Reducing Stress At Your Desk

• Sit at your desk comfortably. If you are at a keyboard, put your hands over the keys. Now lift both feet off the ground. (This is a very simple way to check that you are sitting properly.) Look at what your hands, neck, head and back are doing. Do you still have a general sense of balance? Do you have to make any effort to hold yourself in this position? If your body goes into spasm, readjust your posture until you are comfortable again. Check to see if the bottom end of your breastbone is lifted up, away from your abdomen. Just making this tiny adjustment, by thinking about slightly lifting your chest, can make a huge difference. Do this by allowing your body to float up from your waist. Is there any tension in your back or shoulders? Imagine that your shoulders are floating down, away from your ears.

• When you sit at a computer, your screen should be at eye level. I use an A4 mounted clipboard (widely available from computer shops) when I am typing, so that I don't have to look down at my desk, which would increase tension in my neck. Check that the back of your neck is free by putting your hand there to see if there is any tension. If you have neck strain, this will lead to lower back problems and can also lead to headaches, so it is a very important area to consider. Now check that the middle of your screen is at eye level so that you can look horizontally ahead. Never allow your head to tip backwards.

• Consider getting a special curved, ergonomically designed keyboard, again available from computer shops. This helps you to keep your wrists up as you type and will help to prevent repetitive strain injury (RSI).

EXERCISES FOR PERFECT POSTURE

Lying down on the floor is very good for your posture and energy levels. This is because it helps to free you from the effects of gravity so that the discs in your spine are able to plump themselves up and reabsorb fluid. This is why we are taller when we get up in the morning than before the night's sleep. These exercises will help your back and your posture in general:

• Lie down on the floor with your head on some books. These should be at a height where your neck is free, with your chin slightly towards your chest (leave a gap of 7.5–10 cm or 3–4 in). Lie down in the relaxation pose described on page 15. Now, bend your knees, resting your feet on the floor, a few centimetres apart and a few centimetres away from your hips. Make sure that you are comfortable. The length of your back should be making full contact with the floor. Relax in this position for ten minutes.

- Stand up straight, with your arms relaxed by your sides. Breathe slowly and relax. Check that you are evenly balanced over your feet, not too far forward nor too far back. Keep your legs about hip-width apart and your knees soft. Check that your pelvic area is not tipped too far forward, which can really strain your back, or too far back. Now notice your back: is your spine straight? Try to stand upright without any strain. Imagine that your legs are being grounded on to the floor and that your head is reaching up to the sky. Keep your shoulders relaxed. Check that your head is balanced on the atlas bone, which pivots at the top of your neck, and feel the back of your neck to make sure that there is no tension. Tuck your chin in very slightly towards your chest. The Alexander Technique teaches that the head should be 'forward and up', so bear that in mind. Now imagine that a piece of string is coming up from the ground, between your legs, up through your spine, up through the centre of your head into the sky. The feeling you should have is of being straight – but relaxed.

- From this position, clasp your hands together and take your arms over your head. Stretch right up, as high as you can, without causing any strain to your back. This helps the discs to draw more fluid into themselves.

- Finally, when lifting anything, always bend your knees so that you keep your back straight and so that the lifting force comes from your leg muscles. When you move during the day (for example, if you turn to face someone) don't twist your upper torso. Instead, turn your feet so that your whole body moves as one column.

You should now have perfect posture. Remember how this feels and use it to check yourself during the day, whenever you are sitting or standing.

8

Is Depression Blowing Away Your Energy?

Most people shy away from the idea that an underlying psychological problem may be causing lack of energy. But depression and general unhappiness may be having a devastating effect physiologically. We have already seen how you may be suffering from stress without knowing it, because your body has *adapted* to the stress. Another very common symptom of stress and cause of fatigue is depression. Again, it is possible to suffer from depression, without being aware of it.

Your world may seem hopeless and your outlook bleak, but you wouldn't actually tag the label 'depression' on to your state of mind. In fact, you may actually find it hard to acknowledge that your mental well-being has a profound affect on your physical health. The problem is then compounded because in the Western world there is a great stigma associated with mental or psychological problems, so we tend not to talk about our worries and do not recognise how much of our vitality they might be zapping.

Most people feel low or depressed at times; feeling sad,

tired and not interested in anything, not even in pleasurable activities. Some level of depression is a normal response to many of life's stresses: for example, you could reasonably expect to feel depressed at the death of a loved one or being made redundant. Depression is only abnormal when it gets out of proportion to the event and continues past the point at which most people would recover.

WHY DOES DEPRESSION HAPPEN?

Moods are regulated by neurotransmitters in the brain, which send nerve impulses from one neuron to another. A number of chemicals serve your neurotransmitters in different parts of your nervous system. Normal behaviour requires a careful balance among them, but in depression, a biochemical abnormality takes place. A widely accepted hypothesis is that depression is caused by a deficiency of two neurotransmitters, norepinephrine and serotonin. Drugs that are effective in relieving depression increase the availability of both of these neurotransmitters in the nervous system.

Are You Suffering From Depression?

- Does your life seems dull and without joy? Have you lost interest in your family and social activities?

- Do you find it difficult to relate to other people? Have you lost interest in them? Have you become self-obsessed about your own problems?

- Do you have low self-esteem, feel inadequate and blame yourself for your perceived failures?

- Do you feel hopeless about your future and feel that you can do nothing to improve your life?

- Do you lack motivation? Are you passive and do you find it difficult to initiate activity?

- Do you suffer from lack of appetite, sleep disturbance and lack of energy?

- Do you have unexplained aches and pains?

WHAT CAN YOU DO IF YOU ARE DEPRESSED?

If you think you may be suffering from depression, the first thing to do is see your doctor who may refer you to a therapist if he or she feels that the problem is sufficiently serious. There are, however, many things you can do to relieve the symptoms. The following suggestions will all help:

- Keep a 'feelings diary'. Every day write down how you *feel* about your life, as opposed to what you *do*. You may be surprised at the anger, hurt or pain this can expose and release. This is a technique I use, and I find it amazingly beneficial as it really does help uncover hidden anger and pain that I otherwise would not be aware of. Stored grief, sadness and anger are very energy depleting.

- Depression can happen when your expectations of how your life *should* be, exceed how your life really *is*. Perhaps you need to lower your expectations and learn to accept what can't be changed.

- Consider therapy or counselling. Talking to a professional about your life can be very uplifting. Your energy will soar as you start to release past tensions and current worries. Make sure you choose a counsellor who is accredited and someone with whom you feel happy to work.

- Talk over your problems with a trusted friend or relative. Just talking things through with someone close, even if it offers no solutions, can help. We expend an enormous amount of energy just trying to keep things inside. You may be surprised how much it helps to unburden yourself on someone close.

- Consider joining an adult education class, taking up a hobby or doing some physical exercise. You may find this a tremendous help in taking your mind off your depression. In countless studies, exercise has been shown to alleviate moderate to mild depression, as it releases endorphins, which are the brain's natural opiates, or 'feel-good' chemicals.

- Taking a holiday in the sunshine and getting right away from the daily routine can help you to see things in a more positive light.

- Make a regular time for outings with friends. This will give you something to focus on and look forward to.

- Hypericum (St John's Wort) is a herb that has been shown to be very effective in treating mild to moderate depression.

9

Think Positive

If you are happy with your life, this in turn has tremendous implications for your physical health. If you feel enthusiastic about what you do and look forward to each day, then that in itself will lift your spirits and help your energy levels.

How To See The Glass As Half Full

In yoga, it is believed that energy can be increased by the state of your mind, which should be quiet and positive. You will find all sorts of techniques in this book to help you to be calm, such as breathing and relaxation exercises. However, learning to let go of negative thinking is a different matter. It's easy to write glibly about how thinking positively will vastly increase your energy, but it is actually much more difficult to carry this out.

Two people may have what seems like dire misfortune. They may lose their home, job, partner or get ill. One person will see this as a disaster while the other sees it as a challenge. The one who sees his or her glass as half empty all the time will have less energy than the one who sees it as half full. It really is down to how you think and how you see your world.

Negative thinking provides negative energy, because a thought *is* energy. Thinking creates an electromagnetic connection that sets up either a negative or positive neural pathway in your brain, which then is laid down as a foundation for how you view your life. This is why positive affirmations (where you repeat a particular phrase) can be so helpful in retraining your brain. Indeed, this is such an important topic that it is discussed in more detail in Chapter 44. It really is important to tackle the mental aspects of your energy, as well as the physical ones. A good and happy mental attitude will truly create positive physical health.

Tips For Positive Thinking

- If you are really unhappy about something, try to change it. If there really is nothing you can do, learn to accept your circumstances.

- Remember that you always have a choice. You can choose to be angry about a situation or to try to see it positively. Nobody can force you to feel bad about anything; you are responsible for your feelings and reactions to your circumstances.

- Try to get in the habit of looking at the good things in your life, rather than the bad things. See what you have, not what you don't have.

- Write down everything that is bad in your life. Now

burn the piece of paper and say out loud the affirmation: 'I choose to burn negativity'.

- Next, write down everything that is good in your life and pin it on your wall. If you find this difficult to do, ask a friend or relative to help you. This really works, as it starts to focus your mind on what is good in your life.

- Don't compare your life with other people's. Wanting more material possessions, a bigger house, a better job and so on, will only lead to dissatisfaction. Once you have fallen into this thought pattern you will never be content. Being able to think positively is very much about being happy with what you have and not wanting more.

- If possible, avoid negative people, or those who pull you down and criticise you. Mix with people who make you feel good about yourself, rather than those who drain you or knock your self-esteem.

- If you have a voice in your head pointing out the bad things in life, tell it to stop. Don't let yourself get pulled down into a spiral of negative thinking. Make your unconscious work for you. Always look for the best in people and in your situation.

- Don't worry endlessly about the future. Saying or thinking, 'What if such and such happens ...' will deplete your energy – and is a waste of time. No one can predict the future, and it might turn out better than you imagine!

10

Set Goals and Re-energise Your Life

If you have no sense of purpose in life and have nothing to look forward to, you are going to feel mentally fatigued. Setting goals is an excellent way of beating stress and directing energy and enthusiasm back into your life.

There are two types of goals to consider incorporating into your thinking: short-term goals and long-term goals. Your short-term goals should be manageable and very specific (for example: joining a night school next term to learn French). They must be realistic and achievable. You should set a time limit of around a year to achieve your short-term goals. Long-term goals, on the other hand, may be more difficult and have a wider time scale; for example, within five years. Their purpose is to give you something to aim towards generally, so that you feel you are working towards your dream (eventually learning to speak French fluently). In business this technique is called a vision, or mission statement. In other words, it is about 'the big picture', focusing on the direction you want to take your life in generally, rather than just floating about with no purpose.

In planning your goals, don't set such high targets that you won't be able to achieve what you set out to do. This will just create more stress and tension. Instead, set yourself realistic goals, which reflect your lifestyle.

Use the following ideas to rediscover the zest and interest in what you do. Please remember no one can do this for you but you. You have to make the decision to change your life.

Tips For Setting Short-term Goals

- First, list the activities that make you buzz with energy and bring you happiness and joy. It might be something simple, like a walk on the beach, singing, playing with children or even writing poetry.

- Now, from this list, write down a wish list of at least five things that you would like to achieve over the next year. Most importantly, don't make your list too difficult. Stick to small things, with goals that are manageable. It might simply be visiting a historical site, telephoning a friend or taking up a hobby that you have always wanted to do.

- Hobbies and interests will really energise your life. If you are stuck for ideas, get the adult education brochure from your library and think about what you would really like to achieve. Improving your computer skills, joining a cookery class, learning a language – the choice is endless. Most adult education classes are very flexible so that you can choose whether to study at night, during the day or even undertake a correspondence course.

- If you still can't think what you would like to do, think back to when you were a child. Did you like music, writing or woodwork for example? Have you always wanted to study psychology or painting?

- Now, make that phone call, write that letter or fill in that application form; do whatever it takes to start the ball rolling.

Tips For Setting Long-term Goals

- Think about what you would like to achieve over the next few years. Some people find that writing an imaginary obituary can be very helpful in focusing on which long-term goals to set. Is there something you always wanted to do before you die? Would you be disappointed to have lived your life and not achieved certain goals? Another way to do this is to imagine that you are 80 years old. What would you like to remember that you had done with your life? Or if you only had three years left to live, what would you do with the time?

- Look at your strengths and talents. What would give your life meaning and purpose? What personal abilities do you wish to build on? What do you want to experience in life? And is your life challenging enough? Or too stressful? What could you change?

- Now write a list of your long-term goals; things that you would like to achieve in the next five years. These can be more non-specific than your short-term goals, but again shouldn't be too difficult or unachievable. Taking time out to travel, raising money for a favourite charity, changing jobs, moving house or area, or studying for a degree are examples of the sort of long-term goals you may like to think about. You may even like to consider going back to college or taking a degree via the Open University.

- Don't be rigid about your goals. If your circumstances change, be prepared to adapt your objectives to fit in with your new lifestyle.

Setting goals is something that I do twice a year. I make them easy, for example, joining the local choir or catching up with an old schoolfriend. I check back every New Year and it gives me huge satisfaction to see what I have done. I also regularly revise my goals. Some are not possible or some get tagged on to the next year. I'm not too hard on myself if I can't manage something. Best of all is that my goals give me something to look forward to. In other words, set goals that you would *like* to do, not chores. Make the decision today: it will really help your mental energy because you will have something to focus on and to achieve.

PART II

Overcoming Common Physical Causes of Fatigue

If you are tired all the time, then you have probably asked yourself if there may be some medical cause for your lack of energy. It is impossible to completely compartmentalise your body into 'mental' and 'physical', since what affects you mentally has a knock-on effect on your physical health. A relatively new area of research, called psychoneuro-immunology (PNI), shows that your immune system is affected by stress and other psychological variables. So, if you are generally run-down or tense in the first place, then you will be more prone to physical illness.

At the beginning of this book I advised you to consult

your doctor first if you are tired all the time, as there are numerous diseases that can cause fatigue, including heart disease, lupus, arthritis, cancer, post viral-fatigue and so on. Even if you are recovering from something like flu or an operation, it is normal to feel very debilitated.

Stress was covered in Part I, because it is such an obvious cause of fatigue. If, however, you don't think that stress is at the root of your lack of energy, then you need to look at some more common causes of fatigue, some of which your doctor may not consider.

11

The *Candida* Connection – Gut Dysbiosis

A common cause of tiredness is something called *Candida albicans*, a yeast that lives in the mucous membranes, such as the digestive tract and the anus. Friendly bacteria such as acidophilus prevent the spread of undesirable bacteria and yeasts such as *candida*. The problem starts when yeasts and parasites overtake the friendly bacteria. This is known as gut dysbiosis, which literally means an imbalance of bacteria in the gut. Many yeasts, parasites and bacteria can cause gut dysbiosis, but this chapter will focus on *candida* as it is one of the most common causes of fatigue.

YOUR IMMUNE SYSTEM AND *CANDIDA*

Your immune system helps to keep infections and disease at bay. It is a complex structure, which contains cells called lymphocytes that protect your body from disease-causing organisms. If a wound becomes infected, for example, your cells release histamine and other proteins to fight the bacteria. At the same time the numbers of white blood cells in your blood are increased to swallow up the bacteria. If the infection is persistent, your lymphatic system steps in. This drains your body of fluid between cells and also picks up dead material and foreign bodies. The lymphatic liquid is moved around the body through your blood circulation. The lymph nodes, which are part of this system, produce white lymphocyte cells called B cells and T cells. B cells produce antibodies, which fight bacteria and viruses. The T cells attack infected cells directly by bombarding them with cell poison. Once the invading bacteria, yeast or virus has been defeated, T suppressor cells ensure that your immune system is switched off again and no more antibodies are produced.

Anything that reduces the number of white cells will weaken your body's ability to combat infections, viruses or an overgrowth of yeast such as *candida*. *Candida* is a very successful yeast organism and if your immune system is already compromised, it is more likely that *candida* can get out of control.

These days, our immune system comes under more strain than 50 years ago, as more hormones, antibiotics, pesticides, herbicides and pollution are present in the environment. If your immune system is not working effectively, this gives *candida* more of a chance to overgrow.

Common forms of yeast infections include the following:

- **Mouth:** yeast can cause cracking at the corners of your mouth, a red patch in the middle of your tongue, red, sore gums or inflamed lining of the mouth or tongue with white deposits.

- **Vagina:** vaginal thrush is very common. Soreness, itching, irritation and a white sticky discharge are classic features of *candida* of the vagina. In men, *candida* can also cause a general genital itching.

- **Skin:** *candida* causes nappy rash in infants. Athlete's foot and itchy, flaking scalp can also be caused by fungal infections, especially if you spend time in hot, humid environments.

- **Nails:** A red, painful swelling at the side of the nail can be caused by yeast infections.

How Does *Candida* Get Out Of Control?

Sugar, which plays such a large part in the modern diet, can cause *candida* to grow out of control, because it is a food source that yeast thrives on. The same goes for alcohol, particularly wine, which contains yeast. Simple carbohydrates such as cakes, biscuits and anything made with white flour turn to glucose rapidly in your blood and give *candida* ingredients to live on. Other contributing factors, which can encourage *candida* overgrowth, include: the contraceptive pill, which can alter your hormone balance and allow yeasts to grow; antibiotics, which kill the friendly bacteria that keep the yeast in check; steroids, which may compromise your immune system, and a poor diet consisting of refined, processed food.

You may have noticed *candida* symptoms if you have ever taken antibiotics. Perhaps you got thrush? Or did you notice that you felt more tired after you finished the course?

Antibiotic literally means anti-life, which means they kill off all bacteria – including the friendly, essential ones, so that *candida* can run rampant in your system, particularly if you are already run-down.

WHY DOES *CANDIDA* MAKE YOU TIRED?

When the yeast grows beyond a certain size it changes into a damaging fungus, which puts down roots into the wall of your intestine. It can then multiply throughout your body. This is known as systemic *candida* and can allow undesirable toxins into your bloodstream. There is more bad news. This condition causes your gut to become leaky which can lead to allergic reactions to certain foods and make you feel ill. Once the *candida* has spored through to the rest of your body, it begins the task of cell decomposition. This can lead to you feeling very tired and unwell.

It should be said that *candida* is quite a controversial diagnosis. Not all doctors accept that it is a common cause of fatigue. However, more and more are beginning to realise that this is the case, especially as there has been a huge increase in the use of antibiotics, the contraceptive pill and intake of sugar in the last few decades.

How Do You Know If You Have *Candida*?

- Do you suffer with repeated thrush?

- Are you prone to fungal infections such as athlete's foot?

- Do you suffer with allergies?

- Do you have abdominal bloating, diarrhoea or constipation?

- Do you have depression, fatigue or poor memory?

- Do you have food cravings, especially for yeasty, moist and sweet food?

- Do you suffer from aches or swellings in your joints?

- Do you suffer with frequent headaches or 'foggy head'?

If you have four or more of these symptoms, then you could well have *candida*.

HOW TO BEAT *CANDIDA*

Treating *candida* isn't easy and it will require a radical change to your diet. First, you should visit a good health practitioner or nutritionist who will help you to kill off the yeast with natural anti-fungals. You have to do this slowly, as the *candida* gives off toxins as it dies, which can temporarily make you feel more ill. Meanwhile, you need to cut out all sugar from your diet and all yeast. Initially this includes fruit (sugar in fruit, known as fructose, can encourage *candida* to grow), and cakes, biscuits and sweets. Food containing yeast, such as Marmite, wine, beer or bread should also be avoided. Also, cut back on any processed food. Fresh, organic food is best. Your diet should be based on organic meat, fish, pulses and lots of vegetables. When you have been on your anti-*candida* regime for a couple of months, it is helpful to start to rein-troduce friendly bacteria into your system. Acidophilus and live yoghurt will help as they contain the bacteria that live in your gut, which help to keep *candida* under control.

Often, it is not clear if you have a *candida* problem until you start on the diet and take anti-fungals. As I have already said, you may feel worse before you get better, but if *candida* is causing your problem, then you will notice a dramatic improvement in your energy levels within a month, which will make any changes to your diet well worth while.

Chronic Fatigue Syndrome – Myalgic Encephalopathy (ME)

If you suffer from persistent tiredness, then at some time you have probably wondered if you are suffering from the very serious condition known as ME or Chronic Fatigue Syndrome (CFS). CFS is the term doctors use to describe any fatigue that persists for more than six months. It can include anything from the tiredness felt with depression, through to the side-effects of chemotherapy suffered by those with cancer. The term CFS is also used to describe fibromyalgia, a condition where sufferers experience extreme muscle and joint pain – and fatigue. At the more severe end of the CFS spectrum is an illness known as ME in the UK (Myalgic Encephalopathy) and CFIDS (Chronic Fatigue Immune Disorder Syndrome) in the US. For the sake of simplicity, I shall use the term ME here to refer to the illness CFS/CFIDS.

ME is usually triggered by a combination of the following:

- Prolonged stress

- A viral infection

- Shock

- Immunisation

- Exposure to environmental toxins.

If your immune system is compromised and cannot cope, then ME has the opportunity to take root. It can occur after a post-viral illness such as glandular fever, particularly if you then dash back to work or the gym without adequate rest. In fact ME feels similar to the tiredness after flu. There is literally no juice left in your flat battery and it has been compared to feeling like having a hangover, having revised for an exam non-stop for 48 hours, then being forced to run a marathon.

If you have ME then your fatigue is likely to be so profound that you will be unlikely to be able to hold down a full-time job. In many cases, sufferers are permanently bed-bound or at least partly disabled and unable to take part in social activities, in some cases for more than a few hours, while in others, even talking for ten minutes is too much. Although fatigue is the most common symptom, other clues to the illness include the following:

- Sleep disturbances, such as sleeping all the time or insomnia.

- Muscle aches; a feeling of poisoned joints. Studies show that up to 77 per cent of sufferers are in severe pain because of the illness.

- A general feeling of malaise.

- Brain fog and poor mental concentration.

- The inability to do any physical or mental task for prolonged periods, without relapse.

- Profound fatigue after physical or mental exertion.

- A pattern of relapse and remission. Some days or weeks will be spent in better health than others.

If you think you might have ME then it is very important that you get a proper diagnosis from a sympathetic doctor. In a recent survey held by the UK charity Action for ME, 41 per cent of respondents said that their illness would have been less severe if their doctor had made a correct diagnosis early on. The same survey found that 35 per cent of sufferers waited up to 18 months before they got a correct diagnosis.

Although until recently the illness was believed to be partly psychiatric, it is now known that ME is a physical illness, characterised by a dysfunctional immune system (usually the immune system is overactive and switched to 'on' all the time), which in turn can lead to damage of the central nervous system and the endocrine system, (which is concerned with hormone production).

Professor Leslie Findley who runs an ME clinic at Haroldwood Hospital in Essex gives the following definitions to describe the different levels of ME:

1. **Mild ME:** At this level sufferers are mobile and can take care of themselves and do light domestic tasks. They

may be able to work but in order to do so, they will have stopped all leisure and social pursuits, often taking days off or using the weekend to rest.

2. **Moderate ME:** Sufferers will have reduced mobility and are restricted in all activities of daily living, often having peaks and troughs during the day. They usually cannot work and require rest periods, often sleeping in the afternoon. Sleep quality at night is generally poor.

3. **Severe ME:** This describes people with ME who can only carry out minimal tasks such as cleaning their teeth and washing their face. They will have severe cognitive difficulties and will be wheelchair bound. They are usually unable to leave the house except on rare occasions and will have a severe after-effect from any effort.

4. **Very severe ME:** These sufferers are not mobile and cannot carry out any task for themselves and are in bed for most of the time. They cannot tolerate noise or bright lights.

From this, you can see that ME is a very serious, difficult illness, which places huge restrictions on sufferers. They may never recover from the illness completely, yet look normal, in spite of being very unwell.

Because ME is such a serious illness, it is not possible in this book to go into all the causes, symptoms and treatment. Many of the ideas in this book will help you to better health and more energy, although they won't necessarily cure you. Following a good diet, for example, or trying some of the gentle exercises given in the book, on your good days, may help. However, the single most important thing you can do to get well is to pace your activities. On a good day, don't overdo things and follow the 50 per cent rule. That is: do only 50 per cent of what you think you can do. In this way, you are storing up energy towards a full recovery. Resting between very gentle activity is the key to getting well from ME. Not all people do make a full recovery, but many go on to have a reasonable quality of life, in spite of the limitations of the illness.

13

Under-active Thyroid

As the body begins to age, the production of a very important gland associated with energy begins to fall. This is the thyroid, which is a butterfly-shaped gland situated on the lower part of the neck. The thyroid gland is part of the endocrine system, and it produces and regulates hormones known as T3 and T4, which relate to your body's use of energy.

YOUR ENDOCRINE SYSTEM AND AN UNDERACTIVE THYROID

Your endocrine system secretes hormones into your bloodstream that affect all kinds of functions, including your emotional and motivational behaviour. One of the major endocrine glands is the pituitary, which lies just below the hypothalamus in your brain. The pituitary is often known as the master gland, because it produces the largest number of different hormones and controls the secretions of other endocrine glands, such as the thyroid or adrenal glands.

Hormones are secreted by these various endocrine glands into your bloodstream, where they act on different cells in various ways. One of the functions of the thyroid gland is to help cells convert oxygen and food into energy. It also affects your body's temperature, regulates your metabolism and nervous system, and plays a part in fertility. In fact, there isn't a single cell in your body that doesn't rely on your thyroid hormone for regulation and energy.

If your thyroid gland is underactive, then your system is moving at slow speed. This means that you will have a lower heart rate, lower blood pressure, lower body temperature and a lower metabolic rate. (Incidentally, just having low blood pressure can make you feel tired.)

Many health practitioners believe that hypothyroidism is a hugely under-diagnosed problem. One survey suggests that one in eight of the US population may have this condition. Under-diagnosis may be due to the fact that clinical tests are not sensitive enough to detect it and do not always test for the output of the hormone T4.

Could You Have Hypothyroidism?

A typical sufferer would be a middle-aged person, who is tired, depressed, overweight and who feels 'muzzy headed'. Having a 'moon face' (round face without clearly defined features) can also be an indication. Also watch out for the following symptoms:

- Weight gain that is difficult to shift

- Tiredness

- Feeling cold generally, but particularly with cold hands and feet

- Fluid retention

- Mood swings and depression

- Poor concentration and a feeling of brain fog

- Skin problems such as dry, flaking skin

- Headaches and dizziness

- Constipation

- Hair falling out

- Menstrual problems such as heavy or irregular periods

If you recognise some of these symptoms, but not necessarily all of them, your problem could well be hypothyroidism.

TESTING FOR AN UNDERACTIVE THYROID GLAND?

One of the most accurate ways to test for a low thyroid gland is to do what is known as the basal temperature test. This means that you take your temperature first thing in the morning, which is an accurate way of checking your metabolic rate. If your temperature is low, then this indicates a slow metabolic rate and therefore a low thyroid output.

Using a mercury thermometer, as soon as you wake up, place the thermometer in your armpit for ten minutes.

Write down the result. Do this every day for five days (not during menstruation). You then take the average by dividing by five. If your average temperature is 36.6°C (97.8°F) or below, then you should have your thyroid checked by your doctor.

Your doctor will do a test called the TSH. This measures the amount of thyroid-stimulating hormone in your bloodstream. If your TSH levels are high, then this indicates an underactive thyroid gland.

Ask your doctor to measure your T4 as well as your T3. Some practitioners say that if you are within 20 per cent of the low side of a normal reading, then you may still benefit from treatment.

TREATMENT

If you are diagnosed with hypothyroidism, your doctor will probably start you on a low dose of the hormone thyroxine, or a natural thyroid supplement such as armour thyroid, extracted from pigs' glands. If your reading was within the normal range, but it is suspected you have a sluggish thyroid gland, then your doctor may agree to let you try a low dose of thyroxine, to see if there is any improvement after a couple of months. You will then need to have regular blood tests to measure your TSH levels.

Self-help measures include taking a multi-mineral tablet that includes zinc, magnesium, iron and selenium. Kelp or iodine can be particularly helpful.

14

Diabetes

Diabetes is a disease caused by the body's inability to produce the hormone called insulin, which converts food into energy. When you eat, your food is converted into glucose, and insulin is needed to help this glucose enter your cells to be used as fuel. After a meal, as blood sugar rises, insulin should be released from your pancreas for this conversion. If it isn't, the amount of sugar (glucose) in the body can be too high. Insulin is therefore vital in regulating blood sugar.

There are two types of diabetes:

- **Type 1** Insulin-dependent diabetes is an auto-immune condition and means that the body can't produce any insulin at all.

- **Type 2** Non-insulin-dependent diabetes means the body can usually produce some insulin, but not enough. This is the form of diabetes that is commonly not recognised (it can take up to seven years for the average sufferer to be diagnosed) and this is what we shall focus on here. (If you have Type 1 diabetes you will certainly know about it and will be receiving advice from your doctor.)

Some people may not notice any symptoms of diabetes at all, other than fatigue, which is why Diabetes UK calls it the 'silent disease'. However, early diagnosis is very important in helping to prevent the more serious complications of diabetes, including stroke, heart attack, kidney disease, blindness, nerve damage and possible loss of limbs.

The Symptoms of Diabetes

Type 2 diabetes usually appears in people who are over the age of 40 and who are overweight. The main symptoms include:

- Extreme tiredness

- Increased thirst

- Wanting to pass water frequently

- Possible weight loss, as the body cannot convert glucose into energy, so breaks down fat and muscle instead to try to provide some energy

- Episodes of thrush and genital itching caused by excessive glucose in the system

- Blurred vision, as high blood sugar can alter the shape of the eye lens

- Mood swings caused by high blood sugar, including feeling irritable or having episodes of hyperactivity, where you talk too much and feel anxious

WHO IS AT RISK FROM DIABETES?

Diabetes is generally associated with an affluent lifestyle and is increasing in the Western world. Being overweight and inactive leads to insulin resistance, which may encourage diabetes to develop. This applies particularly if you are 'apple shaped', in other words if you store most of your body fat around your middle. Experts are keen to point out that eating too many sweet things will not trigger diabetes, but there is some evidence that poor eating and drinking habits may be a contributing factor. Stress may also be a contributing factor as it is can make blood sugar levels rise. Other indicators include:

- People with a family history of diabetes

- People aged between 40–75

- Those of Asian or African-Caribbean origin

- Those who are overweight (80 per cent of type 2 diabetics are overweight, although in the acute stage of untreated diabetes, they may start to lose weight, even if they are not dieting)

- Women who have had a baby weighing over 4 kg (8 lb 8 oz)

TREATING TYPE 2 DIABETES

If you suspect you may have diabetes, it is vital that you see your doctor for a diagnosis. If you do have diabetes, you will probably be referred to an expert diabetic nurse or dietitian. Your diabetes will be controlled by a careful diet, and possibly with medication. A healthy diet is one that helps maintain your blood sugar levels (see Chapter 21). The following advice will also help you:

- First and most importantly, take responsibility for your own health. Most people can control Type 2 diabetes very effectively with good diet and exercise.

- Try to maintain the right weight for you. Your doctor will advise you on this.

- Eat regular meals which combine complex carbohydrates with protein. Follow all the suggestions given in Part III, which looks at Nutrients and Food as your Energy Medicine.

- Avoid sugar, sweets, cakes and biscuits, as they will make your blood sugar levels too high. For the same reason avoid alcohol, which turns to glucose very rapidly in your blood and will make your condition worse. Certainly, never drink alcohol on an empty stomach.

- Cut right down on fried and fatty foods such as butter, cheese, high fat meats and cream. Not only will they add to your weight but they also put a strain on your liver. More seriously, they can contribute to the complications suffered by some diabetics, such as stroke or heart disease.

- Take regular physical exercise, as activity helps to lower blood sugar levels.

- Take any medication that is prescribed and keep in touch with your doctor so that your sugar levels can be regularly monitored.

- Keep your blood pressure down. Some diabetic clinics are now advising diabetics that reducing blood pressure is as important as stabilising blood sugar levels because of the risk of kidney disease, heart attack or stroke. Keeping your weight down, eating a healthy diet, avoiding salt and taking regular exercise will help this.

- If you smoke, give up. Smoking is particularly dangerous for diabetics.

- Keep stress under control by following the suggestions in Part I of this book.

If you suspect that your fatigue could be caused by diabetes, do see your doctor. Changing your eating habits from bad to good and losing weight when you are middle aged and may be set in your ways will be difficult, but is very important as diabetes can be life-threatening.

You will feel better and have much more energy if you keep your blood glucose levels as near to normal as possible. Eat a whole-food, natural diet with plenty of vegetables, avoid saturated fat and sugar, cut out salt and take plenty of exercise, and you will be well on your way to controlling your diabetes and regaining your energy levels.

15

Food Sensitivities

In the US, some doctors claim that up to 60 per cent of the population has a problem with food sensitivities, which can cause fatigue. These are not to be confused with food *allergies*. Usually, if you are allergic to something you eat, then you will know about it pretty quickly. Your immune system will respond in such a way that you will have a clear and unmistakable reaction. For example, you may develop a runny nose or rash, or feel very unwell.

On the other hand, sensitivities, or intolerances, to foods mean that rather than having an obvious or severe reaction to a particular substance, as you would with an allergic response, you may suffer with general low health and energy. This is known as a 'masked response'. Sensitivities are more common today because our immune systems have to put up with much more than they did 50 years ago. Pesticides, food additives, antibiotics and pollution in your food can overload your immune system so that it can't cope so effectively. To add to the confusion, the symptoms are often difficult to pinpoint. In other words, you may have a general feeling of being 'under par' without being able to identify the one thing that is causing it.

Some foods trigger reactions or contain substances that will make you feel very unwell. For example, coeliac disease, an intolerance to the gluten in grains (wheat, oats, rye and barley), is thought to be caused by the gluten damaging the intestine lining which prevents the absorption of nutrients. Also, some foods, such as cheese, may contain histamine which causes adverse reactions in some people, making them feel very unwell. Caffeine in coffee, tea and chocolate affects the nervous system, and some find that they are hypersensitive to this. In other cases, sufferers may lack an important enzyme. For example, no lactase in the gut, which is necessary for digesting milk products, can cause an intolerance to dairy foods.

Leaky gut syndrome, caused by *candida* can lead to further problems. Here, the lining of the gut becomes irritated and then becomes permeable. Because of this, partly digested proteins escape into the bloodstream. The body cannot break these down and they cause problems such as headaches, muscle pains and fatigue.

Indicators Of Food Intolerances

Symptoms that may indicate that you have a food intolerance include:

- Emotional symptoms, such as panic attacks, depression, mood swings and irritability

- Irritable bowel syndrome, with wind, pains in the gut, constipation or diarrhoea

- Weight problems

- Fatigue

- Insomnia

- Joint problems

- Excess mucus

- Skin disorders

- Increased heartbeat

- Breathing disorders

If you can identify what is making you feel tired or unwell, this may greatly help your energy levels. However, this may be difficult, as, if you continue to eat or be exposed to a substance to which you are intolerant, your body will adapt and your symptoms will become more vague. To make the picture even more complex, you may find that you are craving the very food to which you are sensitive, I have an intolerance to chocolate, which I love and used to eat every day. If I eat it, I can't sleep, it increases my heartbeat and it makes me hyperactive. I found this out by following a strict elimination diet.

THE ELIMINATION DIET

The best way to discover if any of your symptoms are being caused by something in your diet is to go on a modified food fast for five days. During this time, you should stick to what is known as the Stone Age diet, and eat only lamb, vegetables and brown rice (vegetarians can substitute lentils for lamb).

The most common foods that can cause sensitivities are gluten in wheat, oats, rye, barley, sugar, coffee, dairy foods and citrus fruits. If you feel tired for no reason, it is worth experimenting by cutting these out of your diet. You should then slowly introduce them again, one by one, to see if you feel worse when you reintroduce them. This process 'unmasks' the sensitivity.

For optimum health and to help overcome the likelihood of food intolerances, follow these two golden rules:

1. Avoid putting any extra strain on your immune system, and eat organic foods whenever possible. Foods with additives, pesticides or hormones are going to cause you problems in the long run, simply because of the increased burden they put on your immune system.

2. Rotate your diet by not eating the same type of food every day. For example, don't eat bread all the time, but have days when you swap it for oat or rice cakes. In this way you are rotating your grains, and are less likely to develop an intolerance to one particular food.

16

Mercury in Your Mouth

Do you have any metal fillings in your mouth? Have you ever considered that they could be causing your tiredness? Metal, or amalgam, fillings are made up of around 50 per cent mercury, yet mercury is one of the most poisonous substances known to man. The truth is, if amalgam fillings were being introduced into dentistry today, they would never pass health and safety standards. Mercury is a cumulative poison, which means that it can build up in tissues and organs until it reaches a point when it attacks the nervous system and brain and can give rise to symptoms including tiredness and depression. These symptoms will depend on the individual's resistance, immune function and current state of health.

So why is such a toxic substance used in dentistry at all? In the nineteenth century, mercury in the mouth was believed to be inert and harmless, and it was (and still is) cheap and easy to use. However, throughout the twentieth century, chemists and researchers have repeatedly questioned the use of such a toxic and cumulative poison, until in 1984, an American Dental Association conference in Chicago conceded that mercury might escape from amalgam fillings. Yet, they still argued that this was not in sufficient quantities to cause ill health, except in the case of hypersensitive people. In 1994, Sweden banned the use of mercury amalgams for children and then for all adults in 1997.

The World Health Organisation has set the standard for the maximum safe intake of mercury per day at 45 micrograms. However, according to Dr Jack Levenson, who runs the British Society for Mercury Free Dentists, and author of *Menace in the Mouth?*, 'individuals with an average number of mercury fillings could be exposed to 60 micrograms'. This means that some people may be suffering from symptoms of mercury toxicity – including fatigue – because of their fillings.

Mercury poisoning from low level chronic exposure is difficult to diagnose. Primary exposure to mercury is through diet (seafood is usually quite high in mercury) and through amalgams in our teeth. What is important to note is that mercury has been shown to be continuously released from all fillings and, in some people, this will cause health problems. In January 1997, the British Dental Association issued a fact file on mercury, which stated that about 3 per cent of the population is estimated to suffer from mercury sensitivity. In the UK, this would account for 1.75 million people.

Mercury is liquid at room temperature and it is known that it vaporises at mouth temperature. Saliva, chewing, hot, sour or salty foods and beverages, teeth grinding, and cleaning your teeth can all encourage mercury vaporisation.

The Symptoms Of Mercury Poisoning

The following symptoms may indicate some level of mercury poisoning:

- Fatigue

- Migraines and headaches

- Poor memory and a feeling of brain fog

- Depression

- Anxiety

- Asthma

- Aches and pains

- Neurological disorders

- Alzheimer's disease

Mercury can accumulate in all the major organs, including the kidneys and brain and the central nervous system. Mercury ions can also cross the blood-brain barrier and the placenta in pregnant women. When mercury reacts with red blood cells, it can result in chronic fatigue.

ELECTRO-GALVANISATION: YOUR FILLINGS AS MINI-BATTERIES IN YOUR MOUTH

There is another way in which your fillings can make you feel very ill. Your fillings actually corrode as they are in contact with your saliva. The different metals in your mouth can act as a battery, producing a measurable electric current, with saliva as the electrolyte. So, each filling is like a small battery producing a tiny electrical charge. This current, which can fluctuate according to external magnetic fields like mobile phones, is inches away from your brain (the roof of your mouth is the floor of your brain), and may affect electrical activity in your brain, disturbing the quality of your sleep, and making you feel more tired and unwell. The effects are made worse with root fillings, which use gold or brass screws, and which come directly into contact with your amalgam fillings. Not only will gold or other metal increase this electro-galvanism (battery) effect in your mouth, but other metals touching mercury fillings increase the mercury vapour released by up to ten times.

Symptoms Of Electro-galvanism

The following symptoms may indicate electro-galvanism:

- A metallic taste in your mouth

- Increased saliva

- A burning or tingling sensation (similar to touching your teeth with silver paper)

- Discomfort in your mouth

- Irritability, indigestion and loss of weight

- Neuralgic pains

- Blackening of the amalgam of your fillings

SOLUTIONS TO MERCURY POISONING

First, don't panic. This chapter is not meant to be alarmist. The majority of people who have amalgam fillings and who have a healthy immune system will not experience any problems. However, if your fatigue is severe and if you have tried other obvious routes to improve your energy (such as diet and exercise), then you could consider having your fillings tested by a dentist to see if they are leaking more than is advisable. If they are, you should then consider having them removed by a dentist experienced in removing amalgam fillings safely.

A dentist, such as one recommended by the British Society for Mercury Free Dentistry, will start by taking a full history. Then he or she will measure (in microamps) each of your fillings for electrical activity. This is done using a battery tester and indicates the amount of mercury vapour leaking from your fillings and the effect of having a 'mini battery' in your mouth. If the dentist thinks your problems are caused by your fillings, you will be given a pre-treatment plan to improve your immune function, so that you are in the best possible health before your fillings are removed. This will usually involve, as a minimum, taking high doses of vitamin C, which helps to chelate (bind) the mercury out of your system, and a multi-mineral and vitamin supplement containing selenium. In addition, you will be advised to follow a diet that is as high in fresh, organic whole-foods as possible, and low in sugar and simple carbohydrates such as cakes and biscuits. In addition, you may be advised to take organic seaweed tablets (available from health-food shops), as this also helps to bind and excrete mercury from your system.

REMOVAL OF MERCURY FILLINGS

Your dentist will always remove the mercury amalgam filling with the highest microamp reading first. Special precautions should be taken to protect you, as a lot of mercury is released during extraction. For this reason, a good dentist will use a rubber dam across your mouth and a nose guard, to prevent you from swallowing or inhaling excess mercury. You may also be given eye goggles. You should expect to feel more tired and unwell after each extraction, as your mercury levels will go temporarily higher, however careful the dentist is. You may well be advised to take charcoal tablets half-an-hour before your treatment as it is vital that you continue to chelate the mercury through your system so that it is excreted. Many dentists recommend intravenous vitamin C, the amino acids taurine and glutathione together with selenium, sulphur, seaweed tablets and homeopathic dental amalgam to help with this process. Low heat saunas, steam baths, massage, lymphatic drainage massage and homeopathy are all useful ways to chelate mercury out of your system faster.

If you do decide to have your amalgams removed, be warned that it is expensive. It may also take up to two years before you feel better, which is why it is so important to continue with the detoxification programme after all your fillings have been removed, as mercury takes a long time to be excreted from your system. For further information on mercury free dentists and support groups, please see the Resources.

17

Pollution and Chemical Sensitivities

Smoke. Exhaust fumes. Additives in your food. Pesticides in your vegetables. Mercury in your teeth. Nitrates in your tap water. Aluminium in your cooking utensils and deodorant. Cadmium in petrol fumes. And maybe even lead from your water pipes if you live in an old house. The list is endless. Is it any wonder you feel tired?

Most of us come into contact with some kind of toxin or poison every day. All these chemicals can weaken your whole system. If you are in good health, chemical pollution may have no effect on you whatsoever. But if you are already tired, stressed or ill, you are more likely to be vulnerable to toxic overload. All the chemicals I've mentioned so far can, if you come into contact with high enough doses, damage your central nervous system, your bones, heart, liver and endocrine system. They can cause almost any symptom, from allergies through to chronic fatigue syndrome. Toxins actually stress your immune system, reducing the growth of T cells, so that antibodies are either no longer produced or, alternatively, are produced even when they come into contact with harmless substances, causing an allergic reaction. In this way, chemical exposure may well be to blame for the rise in allergies, including childhood asthma.

There has been a huge increase in the production of synthetic chemicals and our exposure to pollutants in the last 50 years. We can now come into contact with a more complex mixture of chemicals (many of which have not been properly evaluated for their potentially harmful effects) than ever before. According to the British Society for Allergy, Environmental and Nutritional Medicine (BSAENM), there are around 28,000 tons of chemicals used on food produce by UK farmers every year. Five million different chemicals are now recognised, yet relatively few are tested for toxicity to man. The average person in the UK in one year eats 5 kg (2.5 lb) of chemical food additives, plus 4.5 l (1 gallon) of pesticides. In addition to the risk of chemicals in your food, you are also bombarded with toxins from other sources. Examples of everyday chemicals include organophosphates used in household fly sprays and flea treatments for pets, chemicals used in gardening, sprays from agriculture, carbon monoxide from traffic fumes or faulty boilers, paints, glues, formaldehyde fluid used in dry cleaning upholstered fabrics and carpets, cleaning products and toiletries.

Many of these chemicals are fat-soluble and can live in the tissues and major organs of the body, interfering with health. Chemical companies argue that chemicals are present in such small doses that they cannot cause us harm. However, evidence shows that harmful chemicals *can* accumulate in our major organs or fat deposits, until they overload us and make us ill and tired. Many of us have low-level, long-term chronic exposure to chemicals and poisons, which has a delayed effect and causes symptoms that are difficult to diagnose. There is now both clinical and anecdotal evidence linking ill health and fatigue to everyday chemicals, with the risks greatest to the foetus in pregnant women, and to children. Below are some examples of substances that can cause health problems.

SILICONE BREAST IMPLANTS

Until recently, around 8,000 women in the UK had silicone breast implants every year and most were assured that there was no risk to health, that the implants wouldn't leak and were non-toxic. We now know that is not true and silicone implants can, indeed, cause Chronic Fatigue Syndrome. Women are now being advised either to have their implants removed or at least have access to independent advice and counselling before proceeding with implant surgery. Members of the Government Health Select Committee have recommended that advertisements for breast implants should carry health warnings and the side-effects of breast implants should be monitored. If you have implants and are concerned, do check with your doctor or surgeon.

ORGANOPHOSPHATE (OP) POISONING

Organophosphates have been in use since the 1950s. In 1972, OPs were licensed for compulsory use in sheep dip twice a year. Since then, many farmers have developed Chronic Fatigue Syndrome from OP poisoning, either because they have had exposure to very high doses, from falling into the sheep dip by accident, or because they have had long-term, chronic exposure to OPs. Professor Behan at the Southern General Hospital in Glasgow is an expert in OP poisoning and he has shown that certain levels of OPs cause damage to the central nervous system. OPs have also been implicated in what is known as Gulf War syndrome. Again, if you think you are suffering from the effects of OP poisoning do see your doctor and also follow the advice given at the end of this chapter.

Gulf War syndrome

Recent research has shown that members of the forces who served during the Gulf War are three times more likely to be ill than other members of the forces. The multiple symptoms they suffer from include Chronic Fatigue Syndrome. Although these symptoms were initially denied by governments and put down to 'psychological factors', there has now been shown to be a link between immunisations and chemical weapons used at the time of the war, which consequently triggered Gulf War syndrome.

SICK BUILDING SYNDROME

Sick building syndrome or SBS may be caused by a variety of chemicals and toxins in poorly ventilated buildings. For example, mould contaminations from ventilation systems and chemicals such as formaldehyde from carpets and furniture can be recirculated via the air conditioning. Computers, photocopiers and fax machines give off an odourless gas called ozone, which can cause adverse symptoms such as allergies and asthma. In addition to this, such machines attract positive ions (a positive air ion is a molecule of oxygen, which has lost an electron), and there is plenty of evidence that positive ions make us feel tired and unwell. SBS can lead to fatigue, headaches, rashes and nasal congestion, together with repeated infections, as a result of the immune system being compromised. If you think you could have SBS, open your office windows whenever possible, ask for full spectrum lights to be used, and include lots of house plants by your desk to help with oxygen intake. (Full spectrum lights contain more of the ultra violet range and are similar to sunlight. See Resources for suppliers.)

MULTIPLE CHEMICAL SENSITIVITY (MCS)

Multiple chemical sensitivity or MCS can be caused by a massive exposure to one chemical, which then makes the sufferer feel very ill when they come into contact with any other chemical. Examples include high exposure to any of the chemicals already discussed above, carbon monoxide poisoning because of a faulty central heating boiler or pesticides, such as woodworm treatment. This overwhelming contact with a particular toxin upsets the natural tolerance for chemicals, and sensitises the body so that sufferers then react in an allergic way to tiny doses of the same chemical. Worse, sufferers can then become sensitive to a range of everyday chemicals such as perfumes, air fresheners, washing powder or even certain foods. This sensitisation to all chemicals is known as 'spreading'.

Incidences of MCS can also be caused by a low grade, constant exposure to chemicals. MCS can cause an acute allergic reaction such as asthma, Crohn's disease or migraine. The BSAENM call this a type A reaction; in other words, there is a clear, allergic response to chemicals. Masked sensitivities may lead to more low grade, chronic symptoms, which are more difficult to diagnose. This is known as a type B reaction. In this case the sufferer may feel generally unwell and tired most of the time with symptoms such as fuzzy head, lack of concentration, numbness in fingers, muscle and joint pains.

How To Beat Fatigue From Chemical Overload

If you are in good health, you are less likely to be at any risk from toxic poisoning. Nevertheless, we are now exposed to chemicals that our ancestors would not have come into contact with, and which are more difficult to adapt to. The following tips will help your system cope:

- Common triggers for chemical poisoning include a house or job move to a polluted environment, accidental exposure to chemicals or pesticides, decorating your house or treating it for woodworm, or excessive use of fly sprays. See if you can trace your fatigue back to a particular event.

- If this is the case, in future avoid harmful chemicals wherever possible. Use your common sense to reduce your chemical overload. Live in as clean an environment as possible. Don't use fly sprays; use a fly swat instead. If you live in an agricultural area where pesticide sprays are used, close your windows at the time of spraying and don't walk near sprayed crops for a few days. If treating children for head lice, use tea tree oil or neem rather than insecticides. If you cycle in heavy traffic use a mask; ozone and carbon monoxide hang around just at the height of most cyclists' noses. Use household cleaners, cosmetics and soaps with minimal additives, such as Simple or Ecover. Avoid air fresheners and aerosols, and use low-odour household products and paints. (See the Resources for a list of suppliers.)

• Toxins increase the body's need for nutrients. Take vitamins and minerals regularly, as suggested in Part III. Vitamins B12 and C (in large doses) and minerals such as selenium, zinc and magnesium help to chelate (bind) toxins out of your system.

• Regular saunas, massage and even colonic irrigation can help to excrete any toxins from your system faster.

• Treat constipation, as this can cause chemicals to be reabsorbed into your body. Eat plenty of fibre from whole grains, organic fruit and vegetables, and drink plenty of water, to encourage your digestive system to operate effectively.

• Have your central heating boiler serviced at least once a year by a qualified (Corgi) gas engineer, to minimise the risk of poisoning from carbon monoxide.

• Avoid using strong smelling products. If a product has a smell, it may be toxic and you should avoid it, according to Dr Sarah Myhill of the BSAENM.

- Dr Myhill also recommends a very simple exercise known as the Romberg test. Simply stand with your feet together and close your eyes. If you wobble significantly, this may indicate damage to your central nervous system from pollution.

PART III

Food and Energy

It sounds like a cliché, but you really are what you eat. To put it simply, if you want to beat fatigue and boost your energy, then the most important step you can take is to pay attention to eating more healthily.

It can be well worthwhile consulting a qualified nutritionist to discuss your particular needs, together with any specific ailments from which you suffer, and to help you analyse your current diet.

But, even without the advice of a nutritionist, healthy eating habits are easy to put into place. In this Part I show you the basic principles for healthy eating and include some simple but delicious recipes to get you started.

18

Eat Well and Energise

Food actually has its own energy potential. In other words, if you want more vitality, you should choose food with a high amount of this energy. For practitioners of yoga, the energy of food is known as Prana, or Universal Energy. (Prana is a Sanskrit word, meaning first unit of energy, the life force vitality that is all around us.) Food high in Prana includes fresh, whole food that has not been stored, over-cooked or recooked, and that is organic, preferably in season and easy to digest. So the worst scenario would be something that had been sitting a long time on a supermarket shelf, then in your fridge, which you had then stewed and perhaps reheated. In fact, this kind of food would actually *deplete* your energy, rather than giving you more.

GOOD NUTRIENTS

Good food contains nutrients essential for health and energy such as enzymes, vitamins, minerals, amino acids, antioxidants, fibre and essential fatty acids. Two of these nutrients (antioxidants and essential fatty acids) and how they help you, are described below.

The importance of antioxidants

Antioxidants are a group of substances that help to counter-act the oxidising effects of free radicals. A free radical is an oxygen molecule with a missing electron. When one hangs around too long in your body, it can cause trouble. For example, they have been implicated in causing heart disease and cancer. Smoke, dust, dirt and toxins in your food bombard your body every day, causing cell breakdown and they provide a classic example of what can cause free radical damage. Another effect of free radicals is the oxidising of essential fatty acids in your body. So it is very important to stop any excess production of free radicals by eating food rich in antioxidants. These include the vitamins A, C and E, and the minerals selenium and zinc. They are found in whole-foods such as grains, nuts, pulses, vegetables and fruit.

The importance of essential fatty acids

Essential fatty acids are needed for you to have a strong immune system and to enable your hormones to work effectively. They are also crucial for the functioning of your brain and nervous system. Essential fatty acids are made up of Omega 3 (found in oily fish and linseeds), and Omega 6 (found in blackcurrants, nuts and seeds).

THE BASICS OF A DIET FOR ENERGY

You need the vital nutrients from good-quality food to keep your body, including your immune system, working prop-erly, and to give you energy. In the rest of this part of the book you will find suggested daily food plans and recipes, but concentrate your diet around the following: plain live yoghurt, wholemeal bread and pasta, brown rice, meat and fish, pulses, nuts, seeds, free-range eggs and lots of fresh fruit and vegetables. As much of this as possible should be organic.

Most nutritionists agree that your diet should be made up of about 65 per cent slow sugar-releasing carbohydrates, such as fresh fruit, vegetables, pulses and whole grains. The rest should be made up of about 15 per cent monounsaturated fats such as olive or sunflower oil and 15 per cent protein such as fish, meat, nuts, soya, eggs or cheese. (If you are a vegetarian or vegan then you can obtain protein by combining a grain, such as quinoa, wheat, rye or oats, with pulses such as lentils, chickpeas or kidney beans.) If you eat meat, which is a major source of iron, try to restrict it to no more than three times a week and always choose organic and/or free range. White meat (such as chicken) is lower in fat than red meat.

Recently, US nutrition expert Dr Barry Spears has had a lot of support for his claims that we should eat a diet higher in protein for energy. He suggests a diet of about 30 per cent low fat protein, 30 per cent monounsaturated fats and 30 per cent carbohydrates, made up largely of vegetables. In his book *Enter the Zone* he offers very convincing evidence that a diet higher in protein gives more energy, and that, conversely, a diet high in starches like pasta and bread leads to fatigue. I have tried his recommendations and found them to be a revelation. By slightly increasing the amount of protein I eat, and by making sure that I never eat a carbohydrate snack unless it is combined with some form of protein, I have dramatically increased my own energy levels. It is certainly true that the fad for low-fat diets with lots of carbohydrates has meant that many people are actually lacking in their essential fats and are suffering from highs and lows in energy, induced by glucose from lots of starchy carbohydrates. Both these factors will make you very tired. However, the best advice is to experiment and see what mix of food works best for you.

Whenever possible, eat food that is organic and unprocessed, as pesticides, hormones and additives further rob food of its energy potential. Avoid processed vegetable margarines. They contain trans-fats, which make fats more spreadable, but which are difficult for your body to process. These artificially produced oils also act as an inhibitor on your essential fatty acids, which your body needs to stay healthy. A small amount of butter is actually more healthy than an artificial spread.

Your Essential Food For Energy Guide

- Cut out all sugar. Sugar is the enemy of energy as it plays havoc with your blood sugar levels. To increase your energy, you need to stabilise your blood sugar levels (see Chapter 21).

- Cut out all processed foods and avoid food containing white flour, such as cakes and biscuits. Refined foods have been stripped of their nutrients and will be low in energy. They can also disrupt your blood sugar levels.

- To benefit from the energy potential of food, eat it as fresh as possible. Organic, unsprayed and without added hormones or antibiotics is best.

- Eat whole-foods whenever possible: that is food in its natural state, such as raw or lightly cooked vegetables and fruit, and lightly cooked whole grains. Try to add lots of fruit and vegetables to your diet. The jury is still out as to whether cooked or raw vegetables are best. Cooking vegetables improves their digestibility. Raw food is harder for your body to process, but higher in nutrients. If you are eating raw food, eat it at lunchtime when your digestion is at its best.

- Keep your tea, coffee and alcohol intake moderate, because it interferes with the levels of your blood sugar that, in turn, will make you feel more tired.

- Don't reheat food, overcook food, or store it too long.

- Eat three nutritious meals a day. Always start your day with a good breakfast such as yoghurt and fruit. The continental breakfast of white bread, or croissant with coffee is *not* healthy.

- Finally, for more energy, chew your food thoroughly. There is an enzyme in your saliva that helps to pre-digest your food so that you can absorb maximum energy. In yoga it is said that much vitality is absorbed through the tongue. Use a tongue scraper (ask your dentist), to help you to clean your tongue so that you can obtain more energy from your food. Chewing your food properly will also aid your digestion and will help you to maximise the nutrients from your food. Always sit down and eat in a calm atmosphere. Cook your food with love, but remember, these are all ideals to aim for. If you have the odd bar of chocolate or fizzy drink that is OK, just be aware of what is the right diet to aim for.

19

Energising Food Regime

Having looked at the sort of food and nutrients that you should try to incorporate into your diet, you will find below a two-day food plan and recipes that will really enhance your stamina levels. The recipes given here are for one or two people, but if you have more people to cook for, simply double (or treble) the ingredients, and mix and match the food regimes that will suit you all.

Just remember that a good nutritious meal equals vitality. These daily menu plans have been devised with the kind help of Elaine Myers, a health writer, who is an expert on energy and nutrition.

DAY ONE

BREAKFAST

Remember, if you want more energy then you *must* always eat breakfast. Always try to incorporate some form of protein to keep your blood sugar levels stable. Fruit and live yoghurt are good, or try an egg on toast. Try to avoid coffee – it is too much of a strain on your adrenal glands.

ENERGY SHAKE

Serves 1

300 ml (10 fl oz) soya milk or
50% milk and 50% soya milk
Large handful or cupful of strawberries (optional)
1 banana
3 drops vanilla (optional)
1 teaspoon linseeds

Put everything in a blender and whizz for a few seconds.

ENERGY NOTES: Bananas are full of potassium, a mineral that is essential for cell function. Weight for weight, bananas have the same amount of potassium as liver. Strawberries are high in iron and therefore good for preventing anaemia. Milk is excellent for energy and stamina as it is full of vitamins, calcium and protein. Use organic whole milk if possible. Soya milk is also high in protein. Linseeds belong to the Omega 3 family and contain essential fatty acids, which are excellent for keeping your whole system healthy.

MID-MORNING

2 RICE CAKES WITH ALMOND BUTTER

ENERGY NOTES: Almonds have one-third more protein than eggs. Almond butter is far better than peanut butter because it has a higher protein content and the fat in it is of a better quality and more easily digested. Almond butter is available from health-food shops.

LUNCH

A big salad or lots of vegetables with a form of protein such as eggs, fish, meat or cottage cheese is ideal. Don't include too many carbohydrates, such as pasta, as these may make you sleepy. The next recipe includes protein from the tahini paste in the hummus and from the pine kernels. It is also high in fibre.

WATERCRESS AND AVOCADO SALAD WITH PINE KERNELS AND PITTA BREAD WITH HUMMUS

Serves 2
300 g (12 oz) watercress
2 avocados
50 g (2 oz) pine kernels
2 tablespoons walnut oil
Juice of $\frac{1}{2}$ lemon
Salt and pepper

Wash and dry watercress if not pre-washed. Slice avocados thinly and add to watercress and pine kernels. Make dressing by mixing walnut oil, lemon juice, salt and pepper and pour over. (Tastes better if left for an hour.)

Serve with warmed pitta bread and hummus. Use best quality shop bought hummus. (Avoid low-fat versions as the oil is replaced with fillers and chemicals and the nutritional value is lost.) You can make your own hummus by combining two tablespoons of tahini paste with half a tin of chickpeas, one tablespoon of olive oil and four cloves of garlic. Either whizz in the blender or use a mortar and pestle if you prefer a more 'rough cut' version. Add lemon juice and more pine kernels to taste.

ENERGY NOTES: Watercress is a good source of the mineral iodine, therefore ideal for people with low thyroid activity. Avocados, like bananas, are high in potassium. Hummus is high in fibre, B vitamins and essential fats.

MID-AFTERNOON

6 DATES AND 6 WALNUTS

ENERGY NOTES: Dates are very energising because they are high in fructose, a natural fruit sugar. They are also high in fibre. Walnuts are protein rich and, weight for weight, have the same amount of protein as eggs. A snack like this will keep you going for far longer than a biscuit or chocolate bar and should help to maintain your energy levels until your evening meal.

DINNER

As with lunch, choose something with a high vegetable and protein content. For example, choose turkey stir-fry followed by apricot fool, described below.

TURKEY STIR-FRY

Serves 2

2 teaspoons olive oil

2 spring onions, chopped

1 head broccoli chopped into as small florets as possible

4 sticks celery, chopped very finely

2 carrots cubed into small pieces

225 g (8 oz) shredded cabbage

Half tablespoon thinly sliced fresh ginger

454 g (1 lb) turkey strips or turkey cubes (or use chicken)

1 teaspoon soy sauce

1 teaspoon each of fresh marjoram and thyme chopped very finely

1 teaspoon sesame seeds

2 teaspoons spring onions, chopped (extra for topping)

Heat oil and fry onion until translucent. Add broccoli, celery, carrots, cabbage and ginger, and cook on a low heat for five minutes stirring regularly. Don't allow the broccoli to lose its bright green colour. Remove vegetables from the pan and add turkey. If using strips, allow 5–7 minutes. If using cubed turkey, allow 10–15 minutes. If there does not seem to be enough oil, add another teaspoon. Always test one piece to make sure the meat is thoroughly cooked. As soon as the turkey is ready, add the cooked vegetables and soy sauce and simmer for another minute. Remove from heat and add marjoram and thyme. Finally, sprinkle with sesame seeds and spring onions. Serve with brown rice.

ENERGY NOTES: Turkey is less intensively farmed than chicken (but organic, free-range chicken is good). Turkey or chicken are a better choice of protein than red meat as they are lower in unsaturated fat. Broccoli, celery, carrots, cabbage, ginger, both types of onions, sesame seeds, marjoram and thyme are all energy-enhancing foods as they are full of vitamins and antioxidants. Used together like this provides a powerhouse meal. Brown rice is a good form of energy from carbohydrates. Apricots are the best energy fruit available and almonds are the best nuts for energising properties.

APRICOT FOOL

Serves 2
250 g (8 oz) dried apricots
450 ml (15 fl oz) water
1 tablespoon apple juice
1 tablespoon lemon juice
1–2 tablespoons honey
Flaked almonds

Wash apricots in warm water. Mix water with apple juice, lemon juice and honey. Pour over the apricots and leave to soak covered overnight. Next day, put all ingredients into a pan, heat and bring to the boil. Simmer for 5–10 minutes. Leave to cool and then puree in a blender. Serve with flaked almonds.

DAY TWO

BREAKFAST

SCRAMBLED EGGS WITH 1 SLICE PUMPERNICKEL OR WHOLE-WHEAT TOAST

2 free-range eggs (battery eggs are higher in cholesterol and may contain additives from feed given to chickens)

Beat 2 eggs in a bowl. Melt a tiny amount of butter (not margarine) in the bottom of a small, non-stick pan. Add eggs and turn heat to lowest setting and stir every 30 seconds. Eventually the eggs will begin to set. Remove from heat. Keep stirring until fluffy but still moist. (About 5 minutes).

ENERGY NOTES: Eggs provide a good source of protein to start the day. Pumpernickel or whole-wheat toast is high in B vitamins – needed for energy.

MID-MORNING

FRESHLY SQUEEZED CARROT/APPLE JUICE

Mix together either 200 ml (8 fl oz) carrot juice with 200 ml (8 fl oz) apple juice or simply use 400 ml (16 fl oz) of carrot juice.

ENERGY NOTES: Carrot and apple juice are high in antioxidants, particularly vitamins A and E.

LUNCH

LENTIL SOUP WITH A CURD CHEESE, ONION AND TOMATO SANDWICH

Serves 4
1 tablespoon oil
2 medium onions, chopped
2 carrots
2 sticks celery
150 g (6 oz) green/brown whole lentils washed and drained (no need to soak)
225 g (8 oz) tin tomatoes
3 pints good quality stock (chicken or vegetable)
Salt and pepper
Freshly chopped parsley

Heat oil and sauté onions until translucent. Stir the carrots and celery and cook them for 5 minutes. Add lentils plus the tin of tomatoes and then the stock. Bring to the boil, cover and simmer gently for 1 hour. Season. Garnish with parsley. Serve with a slice of wholemeal, rye or pumpernickel bread with curd cheese, onion rings and tomatoes.

ENERGY NOTES: Lentils, carrots, celery, onions, tomatoes and parsley are high-energy foods, packed with vitamins and minerals. Curd cheese is very low in fat and easily digested if you are not lactose intolerant. The lentils and bread combine to make a good source of protein and fibre. This type of meal can be used as a vegetarian alternative and can be served with a jacket potato or brown rice for a main meal. As mentioned in the previous chapter, mixing a pulse with a grain will give you lots of energy if you are a vegetarian or a vegan.

MID-AFTERNOON

1 BANANA AND 50 G (2 OZ) RAISINS

ENERGY NOTES: As before, bananas are high in potassium and raisins are an excellent source of fibre. Both produce a slow-releasing carbohydrate, which will help to keep your energy levels from flagging.

DINNER

Today, try fish pie followed by stuffed apples.

FISH PIE

Serves 2
454 g (1 lb) spinach
Salt and pepper
454 g (1 lb) mixed fish (whiting, salmon, smoked haddock, fresh tuna, hake, etc.)
300 ml (10 fl oz) milk
25g (1 oz) butter
25 g (1 oz) flour
454 g (1 lb) potatoes
Milk and butter for mashing (not soya milk)
50 g (2 oz) Cheddar cheese

Steam spinach gently for about 5 minutes, adding salt and pepper to taste. Line a baking dish with cooked spinach.

Cook fish in 300 ml (10 fl oz) milk. If lactose intolerant, use vegetable stock. Fish should only simmer for about 5 minutes. When cooked, flake on top of spinach.

Make white sauce. Melt 25 g (1 oz) butter and stir in 25 g (1 oz) flour to make a paste. You can substitute olive oil for the butter, if you prefer. Cook for 1 minute. Remove from heat and gradually stir in milk or stock. Return to heat and bring to boil stirring constantly. Cook for about 3 minutes until sauce thickens. Pour over fish and spinach.

Boil potatoes and mash as smoothly as possible. Spread over the fish sauce mixture. Sprinkle the cheese on top. Bake at gas mark 5/190°C/375°F for 40 minutes, or until bubbling.

ENERGY NOTES: Fish and spinach are perfect energy foods. Potatoes are highly glycaemic (meaning they turn to glucose rapidly in your blood, which may make you feel tired). However, when they are combined with a first-class protein such as fish, they help to keep your blood sugar levels stable.

STUFFED APPLES

Serves 2

2 medium cooking apples
50 g (2 oz) ground almonds
2 tablespoons orange juice
Pinch of cinnamon

Core apples. Mix ground almonds with orange juice to a paste and stuff into apples. Put them in a baking dish with a little water. Sprinkle with cinnamon. Bake at gas mark 4/150°C/300°F for 30 minutes.

SUMMARY

These recipes are chosen for their high protein content, together with slow–releasing carbohydrates. This means that you will have more energy for longer, without feeling that dreadful dip in vitality, or craving for something sweet. These are not low fat or weight loss recipes and they don't take into account lactose/gluten/yeast intolerance, although I haven't used any sugar or yeast products.

20

Water, Water, Everywhere

Think of a houseplant. If you don't water it regularly, it will start to fade and droop. Eventually, it will die. The analogy is, of course, obvious. Your body is like the plant. If you don't drink enough water throughout the day you are going to feel very tired and start to droop, or just be unable to do very much.

Two-thirds of your body is made up of water. It *needs* water to invigorate all your vital organs. If you don't drink water you will start to stagnate, just like a pond without rainfall. Water helps to keep all the major organs in your body working effectively. If you are not drinking enough, everything slows down and energy is literally leeched out of your cells to try to compensate. Most people *don't* drink enough. Or they wait until they become thirsty, which is actually too late. If you are not drinking very much, you can't rely on thirst to tell you when you need more water. Consider this. You lose up to 2 litres (3.5 pt) of water a day. More in hot weather if you are exercising. Are you replacing it? Tea and coffee don't count, because anything with caffeine acts as a diuretic. This means that your kidneys are stimulated, making you produce more urine, so that you are actually losing nearly as much water as you are putting in. Alcohol is also a diuretic, which is why you will feel very thirsty after a drinking binge. In this case, you are losing *more* water than you are drinking. Your poor body needs to be rehydrated.

A recent controlled trial of primary school children showed that those who drank regularly throughout the day were more alert and less sleepy. And athletes know about the importance of water. If they are only slightly dehydrated, it will cause a drop in muscle strength and loss of speed. Dehydration affects both body and mind: lack of water actually lowers blood flow to the muscles and the brain, which means you will lack concentration as well as feeling very fatigued. To put it simply: the more dehydrated you become, the more tired you will feel.

Some Symptoms Of Dehydration

If you have any of these symptoms, you need to increase your intake of water:

- Fatigue

- Headaches

- Poor skin

- General muscle aches

- Constipation

- Bright coloured, pungent smelling urine (it should be pale and have no smell)

How To Drink And What To Drink

It's clear that you should probably be drinking more than you are. But how can you do this? And what exactly should you be drinking – or avoiding? Here are some top tips:

- Aim to drink 1.5–2 litres (2.5–3.5 pt) of water a day. The best thing to drink is bottled, still water with a low sodium content.

- If you can't get bottled water, tap water is better than no water. Or think about investing in a water filter to take the chlorine out of your tap water.

- Divide your daily intake into manageable portions. Carry an empty 0.5 litre bottle of water around with you. Top it up from the tap or from a larger bottle. In this way, you won't feel that drinking lots of water is so daunting – and a 2 litre bottle is very heavy to carry around.

- Hot water with lemon is good. Tea, coffee and cola drinks are bad. Alcohol is very dehydrating so drink lots of water after a drinking session to replenish your stores. Very weak herbal teas are all right – but pure water is always best.

- When you start to drink more water, you will find yourself running to the bathroom more frequently. This will pass, however, once your body has got used to its new intake of liquid. You will also start to become more thirsty again as your body adapts to your new regime.

- Thirst is an indication that your blood levels have become too concentrated and that you need to drink. Learn to listen in to your body's thirst mechanism.

- Dehydration is very common in elderly people, who often forget to drink or lose this thirst mechanism. Drinking more will improve the overall health of most older people.

- Always start the day with a large glass of hot or cold water. And if you start to feel sluggish, have another glass of water!

- Do not drink too much carbonated water, as it can prevent vital minerals from being absorbed into your system. It will also make you feel bloated and it is more difficult to drink in large quantities.

- Remember, if the weather is hot, or if you are physically active, you need to increase your intake of water.

21

Are You Suffering from Low Blood Sugar?

Does this describe you? You may not necessarily feel hungry, but if you don't eat, you feel weak, shaky, faint and irritable. Or sometimes you feel so weak and hungry that you just *have* to binge on sugar or carbohydrates, and you end up eating nearly a whole packet of biscuits or three bars of chocolate or even half a loaf of bread! If you relate to these symptoms, then you may be suffering from a very common problem, and one of the major reasons for fatigue. It's called low blood sugar, or hypoglycaemia.

The effects of this condition can be devastating, but the good news is that it is really easy to cure. I used to suffer from this condition. I would literally get so weak if I didn't eat, that I felt as if I would pass out. A blood test showed I had low blood sugar and, with a simple adjustment to my diet, in a week I was cured and had much more energy.

Low blood sugar means literally what it says, that there is not enough sugar, or glucose in your blood to give you energy. The reason for this is that if you eat highly sugary foods, or lots of simple carbohydrates (such as cakes, white bread, pasta and biscuits), then your blood sugar level initially rises very fast, giving you a huge boost of energy. This is why, if you are feeling weak, you will crave sugary foods for the temporary lift that they give you. However, this *is* only temporary as your pancreas then puts out insulin to try to compensate for your high sugar levels, bringing your blood sugar right down. Crash. You feel tired again. And so it goes on. A boost, followed by a crash, as you eat more simple carbohydrates to try and get your sugar fix again. In the end, it can be like an addiction, you literally crave sugar and foods that rapidly turn to glucose in your blood.

SIMPLE CARBOHYDRATES AND YOUR BLOOD SUGAR LEVELS

A simple carbohydrate converts to sugar very rapidly in your blood. Food that does this is said to have a 'high glycaemic index'. Anything made with white flour, including cakes, sugar, biscuits or white pasta are simple carbohydrates. Conversely, a complex carbohydrate releases glucose much more slowly into your system. Examples of complex carbohydrates include vegetables, most fruits and whole grains such as brown rice, millet and brown bread. Latest research shows that even complex carbohydrates should be combined with a small amount of protein to help stabilise blood sugar levels and that using lots of vegetables is a better source of complex carbohydrates than too much starchy food such as bread, potatoes or pasta.

FOODS WITH A HIGH GLYCAEMIC INDEX

Below is a list of foods to avoid if you have fatigue caused by low blood sugar, because they have a high glycaemic index:

- All forms of sugary snacks and sweets

- Cereals such as puffed rice and corn flakes

- Mashed potato (unless eaten with a form of protein, such as grated cheese, for example)

- White rice

- Ice-cream

- White bread, or anything containing white flour such as pasta (this is also better if combined with protein)

- Glucose, honey and malt

- Some vegetables and fruits have a high glycaemic index, including parsnips, cooked carrots, sweetcorn, bananas, fruit juices, dried fruits and mangoes. Only eat these in moderation.

If you look at the two-day food plans suggested in Chapter 19, these are designed to keep your blood sugar levels stable.

The Symptoms Of Low Blood Sugar

As well as feeling very tired, suffering from low blood sugar may also cause you to gain weight as your craving for sweets, alcohol or simple carbohydrates will mean that you are 'binge' eating, and piling on the pounds. There is worse to come. The body responds to this low blood sugar level state by producing adrenalin, leading to raised pulse and blood pressure, and sometimes even a general feeling of anxiety and nervousness. Other symptoms to watch out for include:

- Faintness or weakness

- Feelings of nausea

- Lack of concentration

- Headaches

- Mood swings, especially irritability and anxiety before you eat

- Shakiness

- An overwhelming desire to binge on sweet, starchy foods or alcohol

TREATING LOW BLOOD SUGAR

We all need glucose for energy as our body converts the food we eat into glucose so that it can be used. On a proper diet, if your blood sugar level is normal, this should happen over a period of several hours. So, when you eat, your blood sugar level rises a little, as you take in glucose from your food, then it falls back to normal. The problem is that if your blood sugar level rises too quickly, your pancreas tries to compensate by releasing insulin, to try to push more glucose into your body's cells. In this way glucose and insulin are in competition to stabilise your blood sugar level. If the level is way too high – insulin will then make it fall back too fast.

The cure is to stop the highs and lows of your blood sugar peaking then crashing, and to try to get it on a more even line. You do this by eating foods with a low glycaemic index (as previously discussed) and by combining protein with your carbohydrates. Above all, avoid bingeing on sugary snacks, sugary drinks and alcohol. Also, try to eat at least every three hours, using snacks that are nutritious, such as nuts and seeds. You will find this difficult for the first five days, as you will still have cravings, but these will pass. Here are some more ways to maintain your blood sugar levels:

- Always eat a good breakfast that includes protein and complex carbohydrate to keep your blood sugar level normal. Toast on its own is not good enough; it will make your sugar level drop too fast, and you will feel very tired by mid-morning, which might encourage you to binge on biscuits, making the problem worse. Then you are locked into the cycle of high and low blood sugar levels again.

- Avoid anything that contains sugar or simple carbohydrates, such as cakes, and biscuits, and anything with white flour, including white pasta and bread.

- Cut back on starchy food. This will make you feel tired as it encourages the highs and lows of your blood sugar level to swing. Increase your intake of vegetables instead. Always combine food such as potatoes, rice, bread or pasta with a protein food such as fish, eggs, cheese or nuts. So, if you have a jacket potato, have some cheese with it. If you have some pasta, make sure that you eat it with a meat or fish sauce, and if you have a piece of toast, try cottage cheese or peanut butter with it. If you do suffer from low blood sugar, the Hay Diet – or food combining – is not for you.

- Avoid coffee. It puts a strain on your adrenal system, which can make the problem worse.

- Avoid alcohol. Alcohol converts to sugar almost immediately. If you must drink alcohol, eat something at the same time to keep your blood sugar level stable. If you crave alcohol, it may be because you are suffering from low blood sugar level.

- Physical exercise improves blood sugar level as glucose is used up during physical activity. So do take a regular form of exercise.

- Don't ever miss meals. Eating more frequently helps to stabilise your blood sugar, so you may find it helpful to eat five small meals a day, rather than three big ones. Eat something every three hours.

- If you are overweight, try to lose weight, following a healthy diet. A healthy diet does not mean starving yourself, as you will see in Chapter 22. Eating properly will help stabilise your blood sugar level so that your weight normalises.

22

Don't Diet!

It is clear that the most important contribution you can make to increase your energy levels is to look at the food that you choose to eat.

A doctor friend of mine says that many of her patients are women who come in complaining of constant tiredness. When she quizzes them, she finds that most of them are on a diet and not eating enough. In some cases, they are actually suffering from malnutrition, trying to survive on a few pieces of fruit and a few snacks every day. And many of these women are not even overweight, but have become obsessed with being thinner and then locked into yo-yo dieting and poor eating habits, with diets such as the cabbage soup diet, which exclude certain food groups. However, there are simply not enough of the right nutrients, including protein, in these diets, and many people end up very tired because their blood sugar levels fall too low. Worse still are the very low-fat diets. We need a certain amount of essential fats to stay healthy and to give us energy. Essential fatty acids are vital for your body to perform properly, particularly in producing energy. If you diet, the chances are that you will be missing out on vital nutrients for energy, including calcium, iron, zinc and magnesium.

Most dieters do not make the connection between not eating enough and not having enough energy. Other common visitors to my friend's surgery are teenage vegetarians who simply cut out meat from their diet, without substituting this for any other form of first-class protein such as cheese, or a mix of pulses and grains.

The important point is this: whatever your age, dieting will make you very tired, simply because it is unlikely that you will be getting enough nutrients or calories to give you energy. Women of all ages need to think very carefully before following a restricted diet plan. At any one time, it is estimated that up to 50 per cent of the female population in the Western world is following some kind of weight-reducing regime. However, women need on average, approximately 2,000 calories a day to take in enough nutrients for energy and men need 2,500; any fewer than that and you will feel tired. *A calorie literally means a unit of energy.*

There is more bad news: when you lose weight, fat and muscle are broken down with by-products called ketones. These give off toxins that will also make you feel tired and unwell. So the answer is not to diet, but to think about eating more *healthily* instead. Cut out sugar, snacks and junk food; and eat instead lots of complex carbohydrates, including fruit and vegetables, together with a proper form of protein such as fish, meat or cheese. If you eat a proper, balanced diet, then your body will find its ideal weight, especially if you combine this with exercise.

23

Basic Supplements For Energy

Many doctors and nutritionists still say that if you are eating a proper diet, then you shouldn't need extra supplements. This may be true in an ideal world, but, to be realistic, many people don't eat five portions of fruit and vegetables daily, and often make do with ready-prepared meals. Add to this the fact that many of our crops are grown in poor soil that lacks essential minerals such as selenium. Those beautiful red peppers or tomatoes in your supermarket may be less nutritious than some more unattractive produce, which is not forced under glass or sprayed with pesticides. All this means that supplements, vitamins and minerals may give your immune system a little extra boost to help to compensate for the lack of perfect, fresh, organic food.

Vitamin deficiency is quite common during times of ill health and stress. If you drink a lot of alcohol or smoke, then this can further deplete you of vitamins. If you are feeling tired, the right supplement could make all the difference. It might simply be, for example, that you are lacking in vitamins in the B group.

Remember that vitamins and minerals work in conjunction with one another: for example iron works better when taken with vitamin C; and calcium and magnesium should be taken together. A good multi-vitamin should contain bioflavonoids, which, as well as helping absorption, also act as an antioxidant.

The following is just a general guideline. You should always consult a health practitioner to check your own vitamin levels.

SUPER-VITAMINS AND MINERALS

- Take a good multi-vitamin and mineral tablet every day. See Resources for recommended sources.

- If your energy levels are flagging, consider taking a **vitamin B complex supplement**. (Vitamin B3 will turn your urine yellow, but this is not harmful.) The B complex vitamins are co-enzymes that assist the process of energy production in every part of your body and work together in many biological functions. A dosage of 10 mg of each is probably adequate as taking very high doses of vitamins can put an extra strain on your system.

- **Vitamin C** is excellent for boosting your immune system and is especially beneficial when taken during times of stress and infection.

- Vegetarians or women suffering from heavy periods should consider taking an **iron** supplement. Iron deficiency is a common cause of fatigue. (See Chapter 25 for more on anaemia.)

- A **calcium and magnesium** tablet taken last thing at night will help to relax you, and boost your stamina. People with ME have been shown to be deficient in magnesium. Magnesium is involved in the production of ATP, a molecule necessary for energy production in your body.

- If you suffer from PMS (pre-menstrual syndrome) consider taking an **evening primrose oil** supplement together with a **fish oil supplement**. These oils boost your Omega 3 and 6 levels (essential fatty acids). Evening primrose oil (together with blackcurrant, borage and starflower oils) contain GLA (gamma linolenic acid) which is rich in Omega 6 fatty acids. EPA (Eicosapentaenoic Acid), found in fish oils and flaxseed, is a source of Omega 3 fatty acids. You should aim for a daily intake of 150 mg of GLA and 500 mg of EPA. Three evening primrose oil capsules of 500 mg will contain around 150 mg of GLA and one 1,000 mg fish oil capsule will contain the right levels of EPA.

Note that you may have to take any supplements for up to three months before you see a difference in your energy levels.

The vitamins and minerals listed above are your basic boosters. However, there are many more supplements that can be useful in countering fatigue and you will find out more about these in Chapter 24.

24

Extra Supplements and Herbs for Energy

If you suffer from tiredness, then at some point you have probably looked at the various supplements (in addition to vitamins and minerals) in your local health-food shop or chemist and wondered if any can give you more energy. The problem is, there is such a dazzling array of different pills, all offering miracles, that it is almost impossible to know where to start. Your health practitioner can give you specific advice, but here are the basics to help you select those that will help you most.

SOME SUPER SUPPLEMENTS AND HERBS

- **Amino acid supplements:** Amino acids are the building blocks of protein and are involved in many functions in the body. Many people find them helpful. They can be expensive but you pay for what you get. **L-glutamine** is a popular amino acid for those with fatigue; it can help mental clarity and is used by students as a healthier alternative to caffeine. As well as brain function, L-glutamine also helps with intestinal health and to stabilise blood sugar levels.

- **Chromium:** This is a mineral, which is excellent for stabilising blood sugar levels.

- **Co-enzyme Q10:** This is a natural substance produced by your body, which helps to maintain healthy cells. This helps some people tremendously with energy problems, but it needs to be taken in quite high quantities of at least 100 mg a day, which may prove expensive.

- **DHEA:** This is a hormone associated with the adrenal glands which can help your energy levels in times of stress. As the body ages, it develops lower levels of DHEA. This hormone is not generally available in the UK, but can be bought over the counter in the US or over the Internet.

- **Echinacea:** This is an excellent herb to take in times of infection, as it is a natural antibiotic. It helps to boost the immune system, raising the white cell blood count. Many people claim it gives them more energy.

- **Green food supplements:** These include algae, chlorella, green barley, wheat grass, alfalfa and spirulina. These are excellent to take if you are not eating enough fruit and vegetables, and are usually very high in readily absorbed vitamins and minerals. Good quality green foods can be expensive.

- **Herbal energy supplements:** These can help support the various activities of the cells and body, such as mental function. There are lots of these around, under different brand names. They may come as separate herbs, or in combination, but generally they contain **guarana, ginseng** and **ginkgo biloba**. Ginseng is an adaptogen which means that it helps the body regulate to a normal pattern. It also helps to convert fatty acids in the body into energy. Ginkgo biloba helps to stimulate blood circulation. It increases oxygen to the heart, brain and other body parts. It is excellent in helping with mental clarity. Guarana is made from the dried seeds of a Brazilian bush and is a natural stimulant that can increase physical and mental energy levels. It also has a calming effect, so shouldn't interfere with your sleep. If you are buying ginseng separately, always buy the best quality, such as Korean red ginseng, or Siberian ginseng.

- **Magnesium/potassium aspartate:** (Not to be confused with the chemical aspartame.) Aspartate is thought to increase stamina and decrease fatigue, while helping to remove ammonia toxins from the liver.

- **NADH:** This is a derivative of vitamin B3. A naturally occurring co-enzyme, it helps supply cells with energy. There was a lot of hype when it came on to the market in the UK in 1999: it was claimed it could help significantly with Chronic Fatigue Syndrome and ME. Unfortunately, the trials were based on a very small sample, but it does seem to give some people more energy. The optimum dose is 10 mg, taken in the morning.

- **Noni juice:** This juice comes from a Hawaiian fruit. Many people swear by the detoxifying and energising properties of this juice.

- **Octacosanol:** This comes from wheatgerm oil, shown to increase oxygen to the muscles, which means that your muscles have more endurance.

- **Ribose:** Cells use ribose to convert nutrients into ATP, the primary source of your body's energy. It can help energy recovery in your heart and skeletal muscles.

- **Vitamin B12:** It's worth considering taking this as an extra supplement if you don't eat a lot of red meat or if you are a vegetarian or vegan. Often given as injections by doctors to elderly patients or those with pernicious anaemia. It can result in a spectacular increase in energy.

Note that you may have to take any supplements for up to three months before you see a difference in your energy levels.

ADVICE ON TAKING SUPPLEMENTS

Your minimum requirement should be to take a good multivitamin and mineral tablet as advised in the previous chapter. Because many supplements are expensive, don't go out and buy them all, otherwise you won't know what is working and what isn't. And you will be a lot poorer! Just try one at a time for a few months to see if your health improves. If it doesn't, then try something else. (It may be worth keeping a diary to remind you of what does and does not work.)

All the supplements mentioned above should be available in most health-food shops, but see the Resources for suppliers.

And finally, again, I do advise you to consult a health practitioner or doctor before you spend any money on supplements that may work for you or may not. A practitioner will also advise you which supplements should not be taken over long periods, as they may put extra strain on your liver. We are all individuals and a good practitioner will take into account your personal needs. And, please remember, there is no substitute for eating a good, healthy diet.

25

Any More Iron?

Are you a female, who drinks a lot of tea and avoids meat, especially red meat? And do you do this partly because you think it is healthy? What may surprise you is that the above three factors can contribute to a very common cause of fatigue – anaemia. Anaemia is, put simply, a lack of haemoglobin or red blood cells, which help to carry oxygen around your body. Without enough oxygen in your cells, you are going to feel very tired as all sorts of functions can't take place, including converting your food properly into energy. Even just walking up the stairs requires an additional amount of oxygen. If the oxygen capacity in your blood is reduced your muscles will not receive the oxygen they need and you will feel tired.

Tannin in tea can leach away your iron supplies and red meat is a major source of iron. So, it's not difficult to see why anaemia is so common (especially if you also suffer with heavy periods). Studies show that up to 20 per cent of menstruating women are lacking in iron.

Some Of The Symptoms Of Anaemia

If you have any of the following symptoms of iron

deficiency, it's worth asking your doctor for a blood test to check your ferritin (iron) levels.

- Looking very pale, with pale skin, gums, nail beds and eyelid linings

- Frequent mouth ulcers

- A sore tongue

- Split or brittle nails

- Poor concentration

- Fatigue, especially around your period

Top Tips For Treating Anaemia

If you think that you may be iron deficient, always check with your doctor first, as the cause needs to be checked out.

- The richest natural source of iron is kelp (available from health-food shops), followed by wheatgerm (try it sprinkled on yoghurt), then liver and meat. If you are a vegetarian, it is worth considering taking kelp supplements. Shellfish, sardines, egg yolk and dried fruit are also reasonable sources of iron.

- Supplement your diet with lots of leafy green vegetables such as spinach, watercress, kale and broccoli. However, although these vegetables are high in ferritin, the iron may not be absorbed as well as the sources mentioned above. Over-boiling vegetables can reduce their iron content by up to 20 per cent.

- If you are not a vegetarian, try to eat red meat at least once a week.

- Vitamin C (found in citrus fruits and berries, kiwi fruit and green leafy vegetables such as spinach) helps to increase the absorption of iron.

- Think about replacing tea with herbal drinks that don't contain tannin or caffeine, or at least cut back on your consumption if you do drink a lot of tea.

- You might like to try a low dose iron supplement (no more than 15 mg, as more can be toxic and can also cause constipation). Take iron with vitamin C to increase the absorption. Don't take your iron tablet at the same time as you take zinc, as it will not be so effective.

- You might like to ask your doctor about a course of vitamin B12 injections. (These are becoming popular with celebrities in Hollywood.) They help to increase iron absorption and can also help with anaemia. Taking a vitamin B complex supplement can also help your iron absorption.

It is worth noting that there is some controversy about taking iron supplements. Some health practitioners believe that iron contributes to a build up of free-radical damage in the body. This is why some manufacturers don't include iron in multi-vitamin and mineral capsules. So, if you are supplementing your diet with iron, just do it for a short time (about three months) – and always check with your doctor first so that he or she can keep an eye on your ferritin levels.

26

Detox Weekend

You want high energy levels and a clear head. You don't feel 100 per cent. Well, a quick way to achieve an inner glow is to go on a weekend detoxification regime.

Your body has its own method of detoxification: your kidneys, liver, skin and lymphatic system all help with this process. However, this can be affected by:

- Being unfit, which can slow down your metabolic rate and decrease the detoxifying ability of your body

- Being ill

- Eating poor, unrefined, low fibre foods

- Eating foods that are high in preservatives and additives

- Smoking, drinking alcohol and caffeine

- Pollution and pesticides in the environment

Detoxing helps to give your system more energy to operate as it cleanses your system from inside, enhances circulation and improves your immune system. In a tired, unhealthy body the build-up of waste products that cannot be properly absorbed or eliminated by your body can affect all your major organs, leading to sluggishness, fatigue and illness. Detoxing will give you much more energy so that your body can function efficiently.

In this chapter, I am just suggesting a gentle weekend detox, which is based on fresh fruit, vegetables and lots of spring water. You should combine this regime with dry skin brushing (explained in Chapter 33), which will help to boost your lymphatic system, thereby speeding up elimination of any waste. If you would like to try a detoxification programme for more than a weekend, read *Detox Yourself* by Jane Scrivner (Piatkus Books).

In the programme I have also included a recipe for a lemon drink, which was recommended to me by Dr Ian Hyams who specialises in treating ME and Chronic Fatigue Syndrome. It is easy to make and will enhance your detox process. When you have finished your weekend, if you would like to continue with the benefits of detoxification you can carry on with the drink every other day.

Note that you may experience headaches, a furry tongue and poor complexion during the weekend. This is just a sign that toxins are being eliminated and that the programme is working. You should return to a normal diet very slowly; don't eat huge meals on the Monday. I am suggesting a weekend, as obviously this is easier to do when you are not working. However, any two days when you do not have any commitments would be ideal. Please don't follow this regime if you are ill or recovering from illness, are pregnant or breast-feeding. If you think you are suffering from low blood sugar, then it is best not to do the detoxification programme until you have your sugar levels back to normal.

WEEKEND DETOXIFICATION PROGRAMME

You can eat as much organic fruit and vegetables as you like over the weekend, apart from bananas. If possible, choose local produce that is in season. Try to include linseeds and other seeds, olive oil, garlic and organic lemon juice. Drink as much spring water as you can manage.

DAY ONE

BREAKFAST

Hot water with fresh lemon. Fresh fruit with linseeds sprinkled liberally on top.

MID-MORNING

A handful of organic pumpkin or sunflower seeds.

LUNCH

Large salad of fresh vegetables and linseeds. Use your imagination – lettuce, peppers, tomatoes, herbs such as coriander – your choice is endless! Dress with olive oil and lemon or cider vinegar. An option is one bowl of vegetable soup made with onions, carrots and celery.

MID-AFTERNOON

Glass of organic vegetable juice.

SUPPER

One cup of cooked brown rice and a large plate of vegetables. You can steam the vegetables, eat them raw, or roast them in the oven with some olive oil.

DAY TWO

As day one. When you have finished, remember to eat only light meals for the next 12 hours.

DETOXIFYING LEMON DRINK

1 organic lemon
1 cup fresh fruit juice (organic apple or orange)
2 tablespoons of cold pressed extra virgin olive oil
2 cloves of garlic or 1 piece of raw ginger

Place the juice of the lemon together with the rind of half the lemon in a blender. Add the fruit juice and the olive oil, together with the garlic and ginger. Process at high speed for a minute. Drink immediately.

PART IV

Exercise and Therapies for Energy

In Parts I, II and III we looked at common causes of fatigue such as stress and physical illness, and the importance of a good diet. If you are still feeling tired, then this next part of the book will give you some self-help strategies on how to increase your energy levels instantly through exercise, breathing techniques and holistic therapies.

There are some other therapies that I haven't included here that you may find helpful; for example, massage, healing, cranial osteopathy, reflexology and acupuncture, to mention just a few. There are now so many alternative therapies on the market, it can be confusing knowing what to try. However, I do recommend that you work on your own health first by helping yourself (looking at your diet and exercise for example), before spending lots of money. If you do decide to see a therapist, then just try one thing at a time so that you know what is working, and don't make the mistake of throwing lots of remedies at your energy crisis. You will just end up confusing your body and making yourself a lot poorer.

27

Boost Your Stamina and Get Moving

This is the tough part of the book. If you want more energy, then you need to do some form of regular exercise. It's quite simple. Not only will exercise make you more healthy (and good health is the root of having more stamina), but moving, stretching and weight-bearing exercises will help to convert your food into energy by producing more oxygen to your cells (hence the word aerobic, meaning, literally, increasing oxygen to the blood). There are lots of other benefits. Exercise boosts your circulation, which in turn helps just about every function in your body. This includes strengthening your heart, increasing your bone density, improving your mood, converting your blood glucose into energy and helping your lymphatic system to work more effectively, which in turn aids the detoxification process of your body. Regular exercise really *does* give you more energy, as well as help prevent serious disease.

ENDORPHINS – YOUR NATURAL OPIATES

When you exercise, you produce substances in the brain, known as endorphins. Endorphins are a group of neuro-transmitters that act in a similar way to, and resemble, the molecular structure of opiate drugs. Endorphins bind to the opiate receptors in your brain, producing a sensation of pleasure.

Endorphins have the effect of blocking pain and of producing a 'high' feel-good feeling. People who have the ability to produce endorphins in large quantities are demonstrably better able to cope with stress and depression than those with a lower level of this natural pain-killer.

Because exercise increases your endorphin production, this means that exercising regularly will help you to cope better with stress, deal with pain more effectively and to feel happy and well.

FINDING THE RIGHT EXERCISE FOR YOU

The problem is in finding an exercise that will suit you. It's no good signing up for the gym, if after two sessions you give up because you are not motivated enough to do some-thing you don't actually enjoy. I hated sport at school; I remember freezing days stuck outside in shorts, feeling miserable. After years of trying various exercise routines and failing because I didn't enjoy them, I am now hooked on yoga. Strictly speaking, yoga is not just an exercise, it is a philosophy. However, I enjoy the physical side of practising the yoga postures, which actually make me feel more energised at the end of a class. Because I love it, I have no problem leaving my nice warm house on cold dark evenings to drive to my class. So, ask yourself: What do you really enjoy? Is it tennis? Horse-riding? Cycling? Swimming? Walking? Or would you like the hard workout routine of jogging, aerobics or step classes? Whatever it is, try to discipline yourself to a minimum of three hours a week of some form of movement.

At the very least, if you lead a sedentary life, try to walk more. It sounds like a cliché, but take the stairs not the lift. Or park your car at a greater distance from the office or the station so that you have further to walk.

If you lack energy and are not a fan of exercise, try one of the eastern forms of exercise such as yoga, t'ai chi, qi gong, or martial arts such as karate or kick boxing. They are based on the energy systems that are described in detail in Part VI. This means that you are working with subtle energy forces to take vitality to your energy centres, and you will be conserving energy, rather than using it up. So, you should leave your class feeling thoroughly revitalised.

In the next few chapters you will find some simple, energy-boosting exercise routines that you can do at home. If you are interested in finding out more about yoga, read my book *Beat Fatigue with Yoga.*

28

Pump in Instant Energy

At the beginning of this book I said that there were no quick fixes or magic pills that can give you more energy. Beating fatigue is all about changing your life; looking at what you eat, what you do, how you cope with stress and so on. Nevertheless, there are a few exercises that can immediately invigorate your whole system. These ones here are very simple – but will pump energy into your body helping you to feel more awake and alert.

INSTANT PICK-YOU-UP

First of all, stand upright. Check your posture. Your shoulders should be relaxed. Lift your ribs, so that you are not squashing your diaphragm or restricting your breathing. Breathe out. Now breathe in, lifting your arms up slowly over your head, stretching right up. Slowly breathe out as you take your arms back behind your head and circle them down towards your hips. Repeat twice more, doing the movement in time with your breath, so that you breathe in to lift your arms and out as you drop them. You should be making big circles with your arms, and really stretching up as you lift your arms above your head. Now do this three more times, circling your arms in the other direction. Finally, breathe in and stretch your arms up over your head again. Breathe out. Breathe in, bending your knees and taking your arms slightly behind your head. Now breathe out, letting your body flop forwards, so that your arms swing down to the ground in front of you. As you do this, open your mouth and exhale sharply, pushing any stale air out. It is a good idea to say 'haaa' out aloud, to help force the breath out. Keep flopped forwards, letting your arms swing and everything relaxed, then repeat once more.

Because this sequence pumps fresh air into your body, it is an excellent exercise to do whenever you need an instant pick-me-up. Try it first thing in the morning to wake yourself up – or if you are sitting down working for a long time in front of a computer.

THE HOLY FIG TREE POSTURE

This next exercise is good to do if you feel tired during the day and you want a quick way to revitalise your whole system. It is a yoga pose called the Holy Fig Tree posture and is known to increase energy levels. It is a basic stretching exercise, which is excellent for both your back and your posture in general.

Stand up straight. Take your left hand towards the ceiling and really stretch it out. Now stretch your right hand horizontally, towards the wall. Finally take your right leg and stretch it out behind you, keeping your toes on the floor. When you feel confident, lift and point your right leg so that you feel as if you are being stretched three ways, with your left leg firmly rooting you on the ground. Hold for about a minute. Let your right toe touch the floor if at any time you feel unbalanced. Return to standing and repeat on the other side (see Diagram 1).

Diagram 1: Holy Fig Tree

LOCK IN ENERGY

These next two exercises incorporate traditional yoga 'locks' which are designed to seal in energy or Prana (the Sanskrit word for Universal Energy).

Rowing

Sit on the floor, with your legs out straight. Now, imagine that you are pulling the oars of a boat. Lean forward, arms outstretched and breathe out. As you start to breathe in, pull on imaginary oars as you lean back, pressing your chin on to your chest and tightening your tummy muscles and clenching your buttocks. Hold your breath then release, rowing forward as you breathe out. Repeat this sequence up to ten times.

Pot Stirring

For a variation of the above, pretend that you are stirring a giant pot. From the same position, sitting with your legs stretched out in front of you, hold your hands together with your arms outstretched. Now move your arms in a large circle in time with your breath. At the end of your in-breath, you should be leaning back with your chin on your chest, and your buttocks and tummy muscles tight. At the end of your out-breath you should be leaning forward with your arms out, stretched, over your legs. Repeat for ten breaths, then lie down and relax for five minutes.

29

Energise with the Shoulder Stand

If you want a quick boost of energy during the day, doing an inverted posture will produce it very effectively. An 'inverted' posture means that you put your body in a position where your head is lower than your heart, which encourages circulation to your upper body and head. Put simply, this means that your brain is supplied with fresh blood and oxygen, which will really help to wake you up.

The exercise described here is a classic yoga posture called the Shoulder Stand, which is considered one of the most important and beneficial postures. Not only does it feed the brain with nutrients and fresh blood but, because your chin is tucked in, it will also help to stimulate your thyroid gland, which can also help fight fatigue.

Please don't do this position (or any inverted posture) if you are pregnant, have high blood pressure, heart, lung, eye or ear conditions or goitre. If you have an overactive thyroid gland, check with your doctor first. Don't practise this during the first two days of your period as it may encourage blood to seep into your fallopian tubes.

There are two versions of the exercise given here. One is the Half Shoulder Stand – the next is the Full Shoulder Stand. Just do whichever one suits you best.

HALF SHOULDER STAND

Lie on your back with your arms by your sides and your palms down (see Diagram 2). Relax as much as possible. Breathing in, take your legs and hips into the air. (If you find this difficult to do, use a wall and bend your knees to push yourself off.) As you lift up, support your hips with your hands around your waist. Take your legs and hips

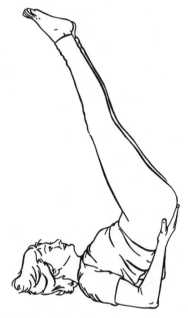

Diagram 2: Half Shoulder Stand

slightly behind your body so that they are at about a 45-degree angle to your trunk. Hold this position, keeping your neck and shoulders relaxed and breathe normally for about a minute. You may hear a rushing sound in your ears: this is the increase in your blood pressure, as blood flows to your head. If it feels uncomfortable, or you feel dizzy, come out of the position. Do this by slowly bringing your legs back to the floor, arching your neck as you lower them. Bend your knees if you have a lower back problem. Rest on the floor for a couple of minutes, to allow your blood pressure to return to normal.

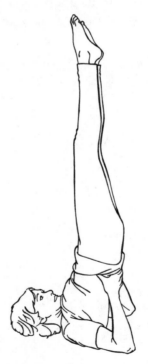

Diagram 3: Full Shoulder Stand

FULL SHOULDER STAND

Take yourself into the Half Shoulder Stand, as above. Now start to lift your hips and legs, so that you move on to your shoulders and so that your spine and legs are in a straight line (see Diagram 3). Don't sink into your hands, lift your back up towards the ceiling. Keep your elbows as close together as possible. Tuck your chin into your upper chest. Breathe normally and hold for about a minute. To come out of the position, arch your neck to keep your head down and bend your knees towards your chest. Roll your spine and hips slowly on to the floor. Rest for as long as you held the posture.

A SIMPLE INVERTED POSE

A simple way to do an inverted pose is to lie on the floor with your legs resting on a chair. You will still get the benefits of the Shoulder Stand in this position, as your head is lower than your heart.

30

Energising Yoga Breaths

The following breathing exercises will help to increase your energy and they are ideal for a quick pick-me-up whenever you are feeling in need of an extra lift. All the breathing exercises in yoga are designed to increase your intake of Prana (Universal Energy) from the air. (You will find more on this in Part VI.)

ENERGISING BREATH

The first exercise is a yoga breath, which helps to combat drowsiness, because it releases toxins and recharges your whole system by helping to oxygenate the brain. It dispels stale carbon dioxide from your lungs so that your blood becomes saturated with oxygen. It also stimulates cellular breathing, which means it is easier for your blood cells to absorb oxygen. In addition, it helps to calm your autonomic nervous system and literally drenches your brain with refreshed blood. This, in turn, detoxifies any stale, circulating blood and also aids your endocrine system, which is responsible for regulating your hormone production. It is particularly recommended for people with ME or Chronic Fatigue Syndrome, because it is so effective in helping blood flow to the brain.

This breath is contra-indicated if you have breathing or heart disorders, high blood pressure, serious eye or ear complaints, or if you are pregnant. Most importantly, return to normal breathing after you have finished the exercise, as it is, technically, a hyperventilation exercise.

THE BREATH

Stand upright, so that you are not constricting your navel area. Lift your ribs. First, identify your diaphragm, just above your navel. Now, pulling in your abdomen as far as you can, breathe out sharply through your mouth. Repeat this immediately: breathe in then out again quickly, using your abdomen muscles to help force out the air from your lungs. The emphasis is on a quick, forced out breath, using your abdominal muscles like a piston. Repeat this for ten breaths and then relax, breathing normally for a count of ten. Add ten more breaths, then rest again. You can gradually add more breaths every week, but be careful, this is a very powerful energising breath.

Remember to return to normal breathing when you have finished.

ALTERNATE NOSTRIL BREATH

This next exercise is a classic yoga breath, which is based on the principle of balancing your positive and negative energies, or Yin and Yang, so that your body feels harmonised and balanced. In scientific studies it has been shown to stimulate the pineal gland in your brain, which, among other things, is responsible for your endocrine system. It also helps the hypothalamus gland, which affects nearly every function in the body, including mood, sleep and temperature control. For maximum benefits, practise at least three times a week.

The breath

First, sit comfortably, keeping your back straight. Place your right hand in front of your face, resting your first two fingers over the bridge of your nose. You are going to use your thumb to block one nostril, and your ring finger to block the other. Close your eyes.

Start by breathing out through both nostrils. Now block your right nostril with your thumb and breathe in through your left nostril, to a slow count of four. Next, release your thumb, block your left nostril with your ring finger and exhale through your right nostril, using the same count of four. Then breathe in through your right nostril, block it with your thumb, release your ring finger and breathe out through your left nostril. This is 'one complete round'. Carry on like this, making sure that your in-breath and out-breath are even. If your hand gets tired, swap it for the left one. Practise this for one minute to start with, then increase the time gradually over the weeks.

Whenever you feel tired or washed out, practise the Alternate Nostril Breath quietly for a few minutes, noting how it restores and refreshes you.

Humming Breath

The final exercise in this chapter is the Humming Breath.

The breath

Sit on the floor in a comfortable position; for example, cross legged, or with your knees bent so that you are sitting on your heels. Keep your spine straight. Close your eyes. Breathe in deeply and hold for a couple of seconds. Now, as you breathe out slowly, hum an 'mm' sound and direct the vibration into the point between your eyes. When you have expelled all the air, repeat five times.

All these breathing exercises are designed to maximise your health, and to restore calmness and balance to your whole system. Practise them regularly every day, and you will start to notice an improvement in your stamina and vitality.

31

Touch for Health – And Energy

Touch for Health is a complete, holistic bodywork treatment that has been developed by chiropractor John Thie. The treatment has become very popular all over the world. A Touch for Health (TFH) therapist will work on a patient, using acupressure, massage and other movements that help the body to learn to heal itself. The simple TFH exercises given here in this chapter can be done at home, and will help instantly to improve your health and stamina.

John Thie developed the treatment by incorporating kinesiology, nutrition and acupressure, into simple exercises that people can do at home. It can be used for all conditions including general ill health and fatigue. I have also seen Touch for Health dramatically improve dyslexia, as the treatment helps to mobilise and clear pathways in the brain. You may remember that I suggested you do the 'cross-crawl' exercise if you have been concentrating for long periods – such as at a computer. If you have tried this simple exercise, then you will know how effective and invigorating it is. The cross-crawl exercise (described in Chapter 7) is a typical exercise that is used in TFH.

The theory behind Touch for Health is that our bodies have an innate intelligence and propensity for self-healing. A TFH practitioner uses kineseology (muscle testing) to show which areas of the body need to be treated. After diagnosing the problem, the practitioner 'reminds' the body how it should function properly. This is done by focusing on the spine, which is the central core of the nervous system, and also by using massage and acupressure movements, associated with the meridian pathways in the body. (Meridians relate to energy points of the body.)

Our bodies hold 'memories'. For example, if you had a trauma as a child, you will probably still carry the tension from that time in some part of your body. This will be unconscious; you will most likely be unaware of the stress you are holding, but nevertheless, this will cause wear and stress on your whole system which can lead to ill health and fatigue. By releasing the particular tension, a TFH therapist is reminding your body how it should be, when it is in good health. In this way, TFH improves the particular muscle by restoring the energy flow, which in turn gives relief to the corresponding organs sharing that system. This has a knock-on effect on the whole body. For each movement a muscle makes, there is a corresponding movement that opposes that function. For example, if you have tightness in your hip, it may actually be to do with a weakness on the opposite side. This may put a strain on your foot, which then affects other parts of your body, including your posture. This, in turn, may then affect some of your major organs such as your adrenal glands. In other words, a tight muscle group can affect every individual cell in your body as one part of the body affects everything else. So, rather than working on the tight muscle group, a Touch for Health practitioner strengthens this opposing weak group. In this way, TFH restores muscle balance for good posture, perfect health and energy. The following exercises are used in TFH to help increase stamina and well-being.

Exercise to Balance your Body, Reduce Stress and Increase concentration:

1. Stand upright. Hold your left hand over your navel.

2. Using your right thumb and forefinger, rub hard, just under the bony part of the front of your neck (your sternum).

3. Now, using the first and middle finger of your right hand, rub sideways, above and below your lips. (So that your lips are in-between your fingers.)

4. Still keeping your left hand on your navel and using the first and middle finger of your right hand, massage your coccyx (the base of your spine).

5. Finally, repeat this, changing hands.

This should be done every morning and any time that you feel lethargic. This simple exercise really does wake you up!

BRAIN ENERGY BALANCE

It is very important to balance the left and right hemi-spheres of your brain, as described for the Alternate Nostril

Breath in Chapter 30. The next TFH exercise helps the brain to co-ordinate the muscle control and activities required in the process of thinking. Try to do this at least once a day, preferably in the morning. Repeat any time that you feel foggy headed or confused.

1. Touch all the five fingertips of one hand against your body, around your navel, while doing the following:

2. With your other hand, rub the two spots located just below the inner end of the collarbone, on either side of your sternum. (The bony, protruding bit.)

3. Keeping your one hand on your navel, take the other hand and rub just below your lower lip for a few seconds. Finally, rub just above your upper lip.

CROSS-CRAWL VARIATION

The cross-crawl exercise, one version of which is described in Chapter 7, is truly effective in helping to re-programme and balance both hemispheres of the brain, maximising the flow of energy from one side to the other. The left side of your brain is responsible for analysing, verbalising and your rational, logical thinking. The right side is used for more creative thinking and tends to be associated with intuition and imagination. Balancing both sides is important. The cross-crawl also stimulates the cerebrospinal fluids, again vital for energy, as these carry oxygen and nutrients to your brain.

This exercise is a variation of the cross-crawl from Chapter 7, which is just like an exaggerated walking movement. It will help to improve your energy levels, your digestion, reduce stress and stimulate your lymphatic flow, which is excellent for detoxification.

1. Simply walk on the spot, lifting your legs as high as you can. If you prefer, you can march to music, to help motivate you, lifting opposite limbs at the same time.

2. When your right leg is at its highest point, place your left hand briefly on your right knee.

3. Each leg must be tapped by the opposite hand to get the crossover effect.

4. Now try the same exercise, but lying down for five minutes.

ENERGY IN YOUR HANDS

1. Take the fingers of your left hand and clasp them firmly around the fingers of your right hand, so that the fingernails of each hand are touching the inside of the knuckles of the opposite hand. Hold for one minute. You will find this very calming.

2. Next, grasp each thumb in turn with the fingers and palm of your opposite hand. This sends energy to wherever it is needed in your body.

3. Now, hold your ring and little finger against your palm and the tip of your forefinger, near the top of your thumb. Repeat on the other side. This helps to keep the mind alert.

4. Finally, take the fingertips and thumb of one hand and press them on the fingertips and thumb of the other hand. Spread your fingers out to make an arch. This helps to improve energy and concentration, and is often seen being practised in meetings!

For details of your nearest TFH practitioner, see the Resources.

32

Refresh with Hydrotherapy

Bathing or showering in cold water is a very beneficial, cheap and simple way of increasing your energy levels, as it stimulates and invigorates your whole body. There is scientific rationale behind this: it doesn't just make you feel more awake, it can actually boost your immune system.

Cold water therapy has been around for centuries and is still a common treatment used in Germany and Austria for boosting stamina and health. In 1993, Professor Vijay Kakkar published the result of his investigations into cold water therapy, which was reported in the *European* newspaper. Professor Kakkar showed that having a series of baths in temperature-controlled water could have measurable benefits for some people with ME or Chronic Fatigue Syndrome. His programme starts with a five-minute bath in water of 20° C (68° F) and progresses to 20 minutes in a bath of 16° C (60° F). This takes place over a period of 80 days. Professor Kakkar's research showed that participants had a marked increase in immune response, including thyroid function, decrease in muscle pain and increase in stamina. This is because cold water therapy makes the body temperature drop, so that when the bath is finished, the body metabolism has to work harder in order to raise itself back to the normal temperature.

Anyone with fatigue can benefit from cold water therapy. All you need to take advantage of this treatment is a bath and a water thermometer, available from any chemist. Below is an amended version of Professor Kakkar's treatment. The water starts at a slightly warmer temperature than that used in the original trials. Take your time before you increase the coldness or time of the baths, otherwise it may be too much of a shock to your system, and you won't feel any benefit.

COLD WATER THERAPY FOR ENERGY

- Start with your bath water at 24° C (76° F). The first day, stand in the water until you get used to the temperature, then very slowly immerse yourself in the water, so that the back of your neck is covered, for five minutes. It may seem cold at first, but you will get used to it.

- Slowly increase the time by three minutes a day until you can spend 20 minutes in the bath at this temperature.

- Now, gradually drop the temperature down to 16° C (60° F) by dropping 20° C (7.5° F) every week.

- When you have finished your cold bath, have a hot drink and wrap up warmly. The benefit is only felt if your body allows itself to return to its normal temperature naturally, so don't be tempted to go and stand by a fire or radiator.

If you have any health problems, do check with your doctor first before trying cold water therapy. This treatment is contra-indicated if you have heart or circulation problems, an infection, are unwell, have severe ME, or have an under-active thyroid gland. If you find that the treatment makes you too uncomfortable, then discontinue the baths. Although many find this therapy invigorating, cold water treatment doesn't work for everyone.

It may take a month or two before you start to notice a measurable improvement in your energy levels. If you do find cold baths are too much for you, try turning your shower on to cold for a few minutes after a hot shower. You will get some of the benefits of cold water treatment in this way.

33

Boost Your System with Dry Skin Brushing

Brushing your skin daily is a very effective way to invigorate your whole system. Some doctors say that dry skin brushing is as beneficial as exercise, as it peps up your circulation and also helps to detoxify your lymphatic system; your body's natural 'dustbin' that carries waste from the body.

You can buy a good quality long-handled bristle brush from any good health-food shop. Use long strokes and always brush towards your heart. Try this every day for three months before a bath and you will really notice the difference.

DRY SKIN BRUSHING

1. Start by brushing the soles of your feet.

2. Next, brush each calf about seven times on each side (front, back and sides). Use a firm, upward direction. Your skin may feel a little sensitive, but you will soon get used to it.

3. Now brush your thighs about seven times on each side. As well as increasing your circulation, this is also excellent if you have cellulite.

4. Gently brush your stomach in a clockwise direction.

5. Now brush your arms, from fingertip to shoulder. Also brush inside your armpits. This is where you have lots of lymphatic glands.

6. Gently brush your skin from your neck down towards your breastbone, avoiding your breasts.

7. Finally, using the long handle, brush your back from your shoulders to half-way down your spine and then upwards from your bottom and up your back. Again, use about seven strokes.

ENERGY SCRUB

An alternative method to dry skin brushing is to use an exfoliating scrub. You can make up your own, which you then use in the bath or shower. Here's how to do it:

1. Mix 1 heaped tablespoon of sea salt with 2 tablespoons of olive oil. If you like, you can add 1 tablespoon of honey and a few drops of essential oil of your choice such as rosemary or peppermint, which are good for energy. Place all the ingredients in a bowl and mix together until you have a paste.

2. Scoop a handful of the mix and rub all over your body, applying more as required.

3. Scrub the paste in large circles all over, moving towards your heart.

4. Now rinse off.

The salt will help to stimulate your lymphatic system, while the honey and oils will act as a moisturiser.

34

Aromatherapy Revivers

Aromatherapy is a very useful way of boosting your energy levels, as your sense of smell goes straight into your brain via your olfactory system and this gives very fast results. Essential oils have been used for healing for centuries. Countless studies have shown that the aroma from essential oils can have a beneficial effect on your whole body, both through absorption of the oils and through the impact of the smell on the brain.

Essential oils are extracted from plants including fruits, herbs, trees, roots, leaves and flowers. These oils are taken from the part that gives the plant its scent, colour and the healing component. Each oil has a unique molecular structure, which is impossible to recreatechemically.

Essential oils can combine many functions. For example, all are antiseptic, some are anti-viral and others can be anti-fungal, aphrodisiac, stimulating, detoxifying, relaxing, sedating or used as a general tonic. They can even alter moods and can be used to lift spirits, to act as an anti-depressant, aid concentration, poor memory, fatigue and to alleviate stress.

HOW ESSENTIAL OILS WORK

The oils work in two ways, as follows:

1. By absorption into the bloodstream. For example, by entering the skin through massage and through the lining of the lung via inhalation or vaporisation. They are then absorbed into the body's circulation system. From here, they can fight germs and toxins. Tests show that, 25 minutes after massage, traces of essential oil can be found in the kidneys.

2. By affecting the brain directly through smell. The scent of the oil immediately reaches the brain via the olfactory tract (which is actually part of the brain) and the smell then has a direct effect on the central nervous system. From this, just about every function in the body can benefit. For example, certain oils can be used to calm the nervous system, lower blood pressure and reduce stress. If you think about smells and how they make you feel, you will see how this works. Some scents may make you feel happy, invigorated or even instantly remind you of a past experience.

Using aromatherapy to increase your energy levels is very easy. All the oils I recommend here are available from most chemists or health-food shops, and there are a number of simple ways in which you can apply the oils to enhance your health.

Recommended Essential Oils for Stress and Fatigue

Here are a few examples of oils that you can use to enhance your energy levels:

Basil is good for mental fatigue, concentration, PMS.

Bergamot is a citrus oil which helps with tension, depression and stress.

Camomile is calming and is excellent for insomnia, PMS, stress, anxiety, headaches and digestive problems.

Lavender is a multi-purpose, all-round essential oil that every home should have. It is an excellent antiseptic, good for acne, headaches and nausea, and is particularly good for stress, insomnia and depression.

Peppermint is good for indigestion, travel sickness, headaches, PMS, colds and flu, and for fatigue.

Rosemary is another essential oil is good for fatigue and can be used as a general tonic. It is also used for headaches, muscular strain and dry skin conditions.

Tea tree, like lavender, has many useful properties. It is excellent for fungal infections. If you suffer with *candida*, you can add a few drops to a douche or to your bath. It is a general antiseptic and can be used for acne, herpes, athlete's foot, dandruff, cuts and sores and even as an insect repellent.

GENERAL MIX FOR FATIGUE

Try this recipe for an instant energy boost:
Mix two drops of black pepper oil with two drops of lemon-grass oil and two drops of rosemary oil. Sprinkle on to a handkerchief and breathe in deeply, or add to an oil burner. Alternatively, mix three drops of basil, peppermint and rosemary oil and add to a dark bottle with a carrier oil. (A dark, glass bottle helps to preserve the oil.) Whenever you feel tired, just rub some of the mixture on to your temples.

GENERAL MIX FOR STRESS

Place three drops each of lavender and camomile on your pillow at night and this will help you to have restorative sleep.

HOW TO APPLY AROMATHERAPY OILS

Most oils should be diluted by a carrier oil such as almond, olive, sunflower or grapeseed. As a rule of thumb, mix one tablespoon of carrier oil with four to six drops of essential oil. You can then use the essential oil of your choice in the following ways:

- **Massage:** Massage loosens up tight muscles and blocked tissues, and also boosts the lymphatic system. This breaks down uric and lactic acids that are not expelled by exercise, and therefore helps to detoxify the body and overcome exhaustion. A full body aromatherapy massage is best done by a qualified practitioner, who will choose the oil that suits your particular condition. However, you can give yourself a head massage, which is also very effective. Before you wash your hair, simply add three drops of rosemary oil and three of lavender to one tablespoon of carrier oil and massage into your scalp. Now, using the pads of your fingers, move your scalp around, while keeping your fingers in the same place. Do this for three minutes. Leave the oil on for half-an-hour before washing off.

- **Bath:** Add 6 to 8 drops of undiluted essential oil after running your bath. Mixing the oil with a little milk helps it to disperse more effectively. Add the mixture only after you have run the bath, and don't use soap, as this will negate the effectiveness of the oils. Use 2 drops each of bergamot, rosemary and basil if you want to feel awake and refreshed, or two drops each of marjoram, camomile and lavender if you want to relax, or just before you go to sleep.

- **Inhalation:** Fill a large mixing bowl with boiling water and add four drops of your favourite essential oil. Peppermint or eucalyptus are particularly good as a reviving inhalation, as both help to clear your mucous membranes, and refresh and clear your brain. Put a towel over your head and breathe in the fumes.

- **Vaporisation:** You can buy pottery vaporisers from health-food shops and hardware stores. In the bottom section, you burn a night-light. In the top section is a bowl into which you put some water, and then add six to eight drops of your favourite essential oil. I use a mixture of bergamot and basil oil in a burner when I am working, to keep me mentally alert. Another tip is to get a small piece of untreated hardwood. Soak it overnight in a mixture of carrier oil and aromatherapy oils. You can then keep the lump of wood in your pocket or handbag, or in your car.

- **Compress:** Take a clean piece of rag or flannel and soak it in a basinful of warm water that has some drops of essential oil added. Now apply the compress to your forehead and relax.

- **Direct application:** Spread a few drops of essential oils of peppermint or basil on to a handkerchief or tissue, and inhale. Or mix five drops each of basil, lemon and grapefruit essential oils and carry it around with you in a small bottle. Again, you can add this to a tissue or an oil burner whenever you feel you need reviving.

Just a few precautions: always dilute the oils when applying directly to the skin, never take them orally, don't use them if you are pregnant or have epilepsy and don't put them near your eyes. If you are taking homeopathic medicine check with your practitioner, as some oils can cancel out the remedy. Some oils are toxic or can burn if not diluted, so, unless recommended above, do check with an aromatherapist first if you are not sure.

35

Homeopathy for Balance and Harmony

If you are feeling tired all the time, you may like to consider trying homeopathy. This chapter describes how homeopathy actually works, so that you can see if it will be the right therapy for you. I also give you some self-help remedies, which you may like to try for yourself.

If you visit a homeopath, you may be surprised at how long your appointment is. A good practitioner will take a very detailed history, aimed at treating you as a 'whole' person. By this I mean that you won't just be asked about your symptoms, but you will be asked about your medical history, what your emotional state is, what foods you like and so on, so that the homeopath can build up a very full picture of the type of person you are – mind, body and spirit. The aim of homeopathy is to create balance and harmony in your system, using remedies that work on a vibrational level and help your body to heal itself. A good homeopath is aiming to get to the root of what is causing your problems, and not just treating your superficial symptoms. It is a bit like peeling back the layers of an onion. As you are treated for one thing, another symptom may emerge, which is then dealt with, until you get to the heart of the problem.

Homeopathy has been used throughout the ages, but in the eighteenth century, Doctor Samuel Hahnemann discovered a vast range of treatments, from which he built up a complete picture of how each remedy would work. He discovered that the more times a remedy was diluted, the more effective it was.

PRINCIPLES OF HOMEOPATHY

- The weaker the dilution, the more powerful the remedy is. Because the treatments are so dilute, homeopathy is a very safe form of treatment.

- Each treatment is individual, so that the whole person is treated, not the disease.

- Homeopathy works by stimulating the body's own powers of healing.

- 'Like' is used to used to treat 'like', as explained below.

Homeopathy works by using 'like with like'. This means that substances are used that, when taken by a healthy person, would create similar symptoms to those of the person who is ill. For example, if you are not sleeping well, you may be given a minute dose of caffeine, the vibration of which 'reminds' the body how to balance itself back to health. If a healthy person took a lot of caffeine, they would probably also suffer from insomnia. Homoeopathy works by stimulating the body's natural reaction to combat illness. So, by using remedies (that in large doses, would produce symptoms of the disease) in small doses, these help the body to cure itself. In this way, the remedy cancels out the symptom.

Some doctors dispute the worth of homeopathy, as the remedies used are sub-clinical, that is, they have been diluted so many times that they cannot be seen under a microscope. Nevertheless, in repeated clinical trials, homeopathy has been shown to work. One of the most dramatic cures I have witnessed was in my mother's cow, Daisy. Five years ago, Daisy had a tumour, which the vet said was malignant and terminal. I recommended a homeopath to my mother, who worked with the vet's permission. With the help of homeopathic remedies, the tumour has shrunk considerably and is no longer malignant. Daisy is now fit and healthy!

TAKING HOMEOPATHIC REMEDIES

It is always best to see a qualified homeopath who can take a very detailed history and recommend the right remedy for your particular personality. There are literally thousands of remedies, which can have different effects on different people. For example, Ignatia can be prescribed for bereavement, but also for loss of appetite or infant croup. Nevertheless, there are remedies that can be bought over the counter from most chemists and health-food shops, that you may like to try. I've listed some below that are particularly good for exhaustion and stress. Take 6c (this indicates the dilution) for most ailments, but use 30c for emergencies or chronic conditions. If you take a homeopathic remedy, avoid peppermints, minted toothpaste, coffee, strong spices and aromatherapy oils as they may negate the remedy. After a remedy has been taken, a slight increase in symptoms may be experienced: this is a good sign.

REMEDIES FOR TIREDNESS AND STRESS

- **Brain fatigue**

  Argent. nit.
  Gelsemium
  Kali. phos.
  Silicea

- **Depression**

  Ignatia

- **Exhaustion**

  Arnica
  Kali. phos.

- **Insomnia**

  Aconite
  Arnica
  Belladonna
  Ignatia
  Caffeine

- **Nerves/Stress**

  Argent. nit.
  Gelsemium
  Nux vom.

- **Tiredness**

  Arnica
  Kali. phos.
  Arsen. alb.

BACH FLOWER REMEDIES

You may also like to try Bach flower remedies. These are the essence of flowers, picked and distilled in alcohol and taken by drops in water or directly by mouth. They are completely harmless, and are suitable for children. There is a large variety of remedies to suit minor ailments including insomnia, colds, PMS, digestive complaints, anxiety and many other disorders. One of the best known, Rescue Remedy, is a brilliant 'cure all' for taking during times of stress. Olive is very good for increasing energy. Like homeopathic treatments, Bach flower remedies are also widely available from high street chemists and health-food shops.

PART V

Energise Your Environment

So far we have looked at physical reasons for tiredness, stress, the role of diet and self-help techniques. However, unless you have a healthy living area, you will not benefit from long-term energy. There could be a simple reason for your fatigue, that you can easily remedy. Tiredness may be caused by your environment, and in the next few chapters we will be looking at how you can improve your living and work place, for maximum health. If you sleep in an area cluttered with electrical gadgets for example, or spend a lot of time working or sleeping on top of an underground stream, then any good work you do on your health will be wasted. I can't emphasise enough how important your living environment is to your well-being and energy, and in Part V we are going to look at ways to improve your living and work space.

36

Electromagnetic Radiation – The Good and the Bad News

At the beginning of the twenty-first century we are all living in a kind of electromagnetic, radiation soup. For example, radio, television, microwave communications (such as radar), power lines and cables are just about everywhere on our planet. One estimate is that the world is now covered with radio frequency waves, which are 100 to 200 million times stronger than the levels reaching us naturally from the sun.

There is increasing evidence that strong electrical fields may well cause ill health and fatigue. Every source of electricity produces invisible electromagnetic fields (EMFs), which are weak or strong, according to the current involved, and dependent on whether the electricity passes through coils. Transformers, motors, some areas in trains, microwave ovens and mobile or cordless phones can all give off high levels of electromagnetic radiation.

How EMFs Are Measured

We give off weak electromagnetic fields ourselves. Your brain waves can be measured in Hertz (cycles per second), and Hertz is used to measure the particular electromagnetic *frequency*, or vibration. Mains electricity in your house radiates electrical magnetic fields at a *frequency* of 50 or 60 Hertz, depending on which part of the world you live in. (In the UK, this is 50 and in the US, 60 Hertz.) It has been suggested that a constant 50 Hertz resonates in the body in a way that may cause problems for some people. Research has also shown that humans are adversely affected by *very low frequencies*, such as are given out by power lines, as well as by *very high frequencies*, such a microwaves, radar, communications transmitters and X-rays.

The *strength* of a particular EMF is measured in Teslas or Gauss. If the field strength is strong, combined with the Hertz being at a certain frequency, then this may cause health problems. It is also thought that continuous exposure to low field strengths can also cause health problems.

Pulsed electromagnetic waves are produced by electricity flowing in wires and cables, or generated by electrical equipment. These can be measured by an oscilloscope. To add to this, there is AC (alternating current) and DC (direct current). AC does not flow steadily, but changes direction with the effect of pulsing, and it is the electromagnetic field produced by these AC changes that may contribute to poor health. Research has also shown that if we are exposed to electromagnetic fields that produce a steady waveform, these are more likely to be harmful than intermittent exposure to a pattern of changing frequencies. For example, a hairdryer produces an electromagnetic field with a high Gauss reading, as does an electric toothbrush. However, because you use them for a short amount of time, they are less harmful than equipment that you might have in your bedroom to which you are continuously exposed. For this reason, you need to consider the electrical equipment around your bed, as you are likely to be in contact with this particular field for around eight hours at a time.

Electromagnetic fields are strongest (i.e. have a higher Gauss reading) when wire is coiled. So a coiled wire will magnify radiation perhaps 100 fold, regardless of current. Also, electromagnetic radiation becomes weaker with the distance you are from it. So your clock radio, computer or any other household appliance will be safer the further away you are from its transformer. Manufacturers are aware of the danger of this to us and to other functions of their equipment, so, fortunately, most hazardous components are becoming safer and better shielded. However, one of the most questionable home appliances in terms of health is the microwave oven. This has to give out very high radiation, or it wouldn't cook food, so never stand in front of one when it's switched on!

Alzheimer's disease, cancer, MS, Chronic Fatigue Syndrome, insomnia and stress have all been linked to constant exposure to EMFs. At the very least, being in constant contact with certain types of electromagnetic fields can make you unwell and tired, particularly if you are exposed to certain types of equipment for long periods of time.

The Symptoms Of Electromagnetic Stress

The following symptoms may indicate that you are suffering from electromagnetic-induced stress:

- Feeling tired all the time, even when you wake up

- Insomnia or poor quality sleep, as your brain is continuously stimulated by electromagnetic fields

- Stress

- Allergies

- Problems with concentration

- Hyperactivity in children

TAKING ACTION TO IMPROVE YOUR ELECTRICAL ENVIRONMENT

Below is a list of simple solutions to the problem of over-exposure to electromagnetic radiation:

- Remember, electromagnetic fields become exponentially weaker with distance, so use your common sense. The appliances that give off the most harmful radiation include clock radios, electric blankets, televisions and microwaves. Electric blankets contain loops of wires, so are particularly problematical. If you have any of this equipment in your bedroom, move it so that it is not near your head or pull out the plug at night. (Just turning the appliance off is not enough: the plug should actually be disconnected, as live flexes give off EMFs.)

- Check where you sleep. Make sure that you are not sleeping above or behind the fuse box or burglar alarm, or any kind of circuit board. Don't sleep near a satellite dish. If you have one on your roof, make sure that you are not directly under it, particularly if you have a flat roof. If you sleep behind a partition wall, you may like to investigate to see if your neighbours have any electrical equipment near your head. Move your bed if necessary. Don't place your bed too near to a metal radiator, as they can conduct EMFs.

- Metal bed frames can conduct EMFs, and sprung mattresses can increase the field because of the coils involved. There is evidence to suggest that springs can focus and magnify the earth's magnetic field, which could prove harmful. If possible, sleep on a wooden slatted bed and don't use a mattress with springs.

- Don't stand or sit near electrical equipment for long periods of time. Be at least 1 m (3 ft) away. Modern computer screens have now been designed to emit only low radiation, but sit as far away from your screen as you can and take frequent breaks away from your computer. The radiation levels are stronger at the back of a computer, so avoid sitting for long periods behind any computer. Sit at least 3–4 m (10–12 ft) from your television set. New 'Internet equipped' televisions still need to be viewed at a distance; their radiation shielding is nothing like as effective as a modern computer screen.

- Beware of microwave ovens. I have measured one with my own milli-Gauss meter and found that even in the next room, the microwave oven still emitted unacceptably high levels of EMFs. Either don't use a microwave oven at all, or stand well away from it, particularly if you are pregnant.

• Be aware that the debate about whether mobile phones cause harm or not is still raging. There is no doubt that when a mobile phone is pressed to your ear, it emits a high dose of electromagnetic radiation, and some research shows that this can cause 'hot spots' in the brain, or even leakage into the blood-brain barrier. Use landlines where possible and advise teenagers to send text-messages rather than using their phone for talking for long periods.

• Ensure that your electrical equipment and wiring is checked regularly. For example, microwave ovens should be tested to make sure that they are not leaking.

• If you are buying a house, consider your environment. It is probably not advisable to move too close to overhead power lines, railway lines, substations or pylons.

• Experts suggest that close exposure to the following electrical equipment should be limited: televisions, visual display units, radio clocks, electric blankets, fires and fans, metal-based lamps, storage heaters, shaver sockets, fish tank pumps, battery charging units, control boxes for train sets, and stand-alone low voltage halogen spotlights with their own built-in transformer. If in doubt, buy a milli-Gauss meter, such as the Coghill Field Mouse, and check for yourself! (See Resources for further details.) I have my own hand-held meter, which I always take when I travel, so that I can check the bedroom and see where the best place to sleep is.

THE GOOD NEWS

Electromagnetic radiation can be both harmful and beneficial for health and energy. As we have seen, all electricity has a *magnetic* force. What this means is that any *moving* magnetic field induces an AC (alternating) electrical current. All of us rely on our own internal electromagnetic fields to control everything in the body, such as heartbeat, brainwaves and nerve impulses. Every cell needs the successful transmission of electrical charges, which is essential to all bodily functions.

Research has shown that healers generate particular electromagnetic frequencies, which can have a beneficial effect on the human body. These frequencies are around 8–9 Hertz, similar to the magnetic frequency of the earth. Recently, electromagnetic devices have come on to the market, which use these beneficial frequencies to help with healing.

Stephen Walpole, an inventor and software designer, invented such a device after suffering from severe migraines following an accident. He developed a brain frequency analyser, which measures brain waves from 0.5 Hertz to 15 Hertz. From this, the analyser identifies which brain waves may be missing or underpowered, due to ill health. After investigations and controlled trials, Walpole isolated the brain frequencies that relate to migraines. He then developed a small, battery-powered device with a microprocessor, which, when worn continuously, filled in the missing pulses. Up to 70 per cent of those who wore the device during trials (marketed as Empulse and Trimed) reported an improvement in the reduction of migraines.

More recently, Walpole isolated missing brain frequencies relating to insomnia, stress and fatigue. For example, those who suffer from stress may show gaps in the Alpha frequency range, from 9–12 Hertz, which relate to relaxation. By filling in the missing pulses, stress can then be alleviated. I wear the Trimed device, and found it invaluable when I suffered from insomnia. I now continue to wear the device for increased energy.

Another, similar device called the Aegis pendant, pulses between 0.5 Hertz and 15.2 Hertz in changing patterns, over a 28-day cycle. The Aegis creates a weak (and beneficial) electromagnetic field, compatible with the human brain, which seems to help with general health, including problems with stress. (Details of all these devices are given in the Resources.)

Using magnets with a *static* magnetic force (DC, or direct current, but without electricity), can also have a positive effect on health, and in the next chapter we will be exploring ways in which you can use static magnets to increase your energy.

37

Magnet Therapy

Like pulsed, electromagnetic devices, static magnets can also be beneficial for your health and can be used to boost energy. The earth has a natural magnetic force, which is essential to human health. This resonates at a frequency of around 7.8 Hertz. All living creatures are sensitive to this magnetic field. For example, birds migrating south for the winter have been shown to rely on an internal compass to direct them. Evidence has shown that our bodies work best when our own electromagnetic field is in harmony with the planet's magnetic force. For instance, astronauts on early expeditions suffered from immune problems, neurological disturbances and bone disorders such as osteoporosis because of being away from this magnetic field. Now, space programmes incorporate magnets in astronauts' suits to replicate the earth's force and to prevent such health problems occurring.

The first naturally occurring magnet that was discovered centuries ago was the natural mineral lodestone, an iron-rich ore that becomes magnetised through exposure to the earth's magnetic field. From this, our ancestors discovered that magnets had a healing property that could be used to control pain and increase general health and energy. In medieval times, magnets were placed directly on parts of the body to induce healing.

Magnets are still used today for healing and energy. Understanding how magnetism works is quite complex, but, put simply, a magnet is made of unpaired electrons that have the same direction of 'spin', and a magnetic field forces unpaired electrons to line up and spin in the same direction. (Either north or south.) You may remember from science lessons at school that 'unlike' poles (north and south) attract, and 'like' poles repel. This static, magnetic field gives out a strength, which can be measured (like an electromagnetic field) in Teslas or Gauss. Magnets used in healing usually have strengths of between 200–2000 Gauss.

WHY ARE MAGNETS GOOD FOR HEALTH?

A magnetic field affects the positive iron atom in your red blood cells, enabling them to carry more oxygen to the muscles. This means that wearing a therapeutic magnet may help with blood flow and circulation, can help carry oxygen and nutrients more effectively to all your tissues, and can also aid in carrying waste products out of your body faster via your lungs and kidneys. Trials have shown that magnetic fields may redress any imbalance of your own weakened electromagnetic field, which may be caused by ill health. Various controlled studies have shown that oxygen absorption is increased when a magnet is placed near the relevant part of the body, and this may reduce pain and increase energy. So, a static magnetic field helps the blood to carry oxygen to muscle tissues, helping them to gain energy, so that they can work for longer, before they get tired.

Magnets also affect enzymes in the body. Enzymes are proteins, which act as catalysts, either speeding up, or slowing down our reactions. Magnetic fields appear to help this process. In studies, magnets have also been shown to increase the levels of feel-good, opiate-type endorphins by up to 25 per cent. In addition to all this, magnets appear to balance the pH of the blood (the alkaline/acid balance which needs to be regulated at 7.4 for good health). In doing this, magnets can help to remove the build up of lactic acids and other waste products in the body and provide the right environment for aerobic oxidation.

In short, being exposed to a static magnetic field speeds up or slows down the chemical reactions in your body to their optimum levels, and has a stabilising and balancing effect. This means that wearing a magnet for short periods of time can help with blood circulation, healing, fluid retention, detoxification and energy.

How To Choose Magnets For Energy

There are literally hundreds of types of magnets on the market. Most are inexpensive and range from bracelets that you can wear on your wrist, to mattresses treated with magnetic particles, socks for aching feet, or plain magnets that you can place on aching joints. In the Resources, I list some good suppliers.

Magnets range in field strength, and the strongest is not always the best. A good therapist will be able to advise which is suitable for you. Most therapists agree that magnets shouldn't be worn constantly, no more than eight hours at a time for a period of one to two months. This is in order for the body to be able to heal naturally, after the magnet is taken off. The magnet can then be used again, in times of ill health or fatigue. Magnets are contra-indicated if you are wearing a pacemaker, are pregnant, or have a blood clotting problem.

MAGNETISED ENERGY DRINK

Drinking magnetised water (water treated by exposing it to a magnetic field) is a simple and cheap way to increase your health and energy. For this, you can use tap or bottled water. Simply place two strong magnets on a glass or jug of water, one on either side, with the opposite poles facing inwards. (These are the poles, which attract one another.) Tape the magnets to the container. Leave for at least one hour, or preferably overnight. Drink first thing in the morning for optimum results. Don't put the container near any electromagnetic field such as the microwave, kettle or fridge.

After drinking magnetised water for a month, you should notice an increase in your vitality levels. You can also use magnetised water for your plants or for pets' drinking water.

38

Geopathic Stress

We have seen how the influence of the earth's energies has a huge effect on your health. The earth has a weak magnetic field, which has a biological impact on everyone, and this can be beneficial or detrimental. Magnetic waves from the stratosphere affect the surface of the earth, encircling it from north to south and east to west. This 'grid' pattern was first discovered by a scientist called Ernst Hartmann in the last century and is called the Hartmann Grid. Another scientist, Manfred Curry, discovered a second magnetic energy field, which originates from the earth's magnetic core. This is called the Curry Grid and runs diagonal to the Hartmann Grid. The lines of both grids rise vertically, and alternate with positive and negative magnetism. These grid systems can cause problems when they cross over, or intersect, as they create a disturbed magnetic field (such as you get when two magnets repel each other). Interestingly, just before an earthquake, the Hartmann Grid becomes distorted. Some scientists have shown that being exposed for long periods to these disturbed fields may lead to health problems, including fatigue.

Dr Hartmann researched the effects of the earth's magnetic field on humans over a period of 30 years. He suggested that disease is a problem of location and that those who live in areas of geopathic disturbance suffer from immune problems that may make them less able to defend themselves against viruses or bacteria in the normal way. Other studies have shown an interaction between magnetic fields and human biological systems, which affect the oxidation process in the body, and which can lead to damage to the immune and endocrine systems. This means that geopathic stress is thought to cause problems to the body's electrical-magnetic balance and cell metabolism.

Other factors can add to this 'geopathic stress' effect on the body. For example, underground water in rivers and streams is a source of harmful radiation, as the water creates an electromagnetic field, which can, in turn, disturb our own electromagnetic fields. This happens because the water flow is enclosed, which creates electromagnetic radiation, as electrons are knocked off the water molecule through friction. These fields can build up to very high levels.

Mining, excavations, excessive building works, mineral deposits such as coal, caves, the underground tube system, underground fault lines and sewers can all add to geopathic stress, as they interfere with and distort the earth's natural magnetic grid lines. The wavelength of the natural radiation, thus changed, becomes harmful to living organisms. To add to the problem, geopathic stress is thought to increase the effects of EMFs caused by electricity and electrical equipment.

WHAT CAUSES GEOPATHIC STRESS?

If you spend much time living, sleeping or working in an

area of geopathic stress, then it may cause you eventually to become ill. The following may cause problems:

- Being above an underground stream

- Being near power cables, television or mobile phone repeater mast, near a power station or other strong electromagnetic fields, combined with being in an area of geopathic stress

- Being downstream of polluted rivers or canals

- Being above underground caverns, mines, or cavities such as tunnels, which may have distorted the earth's natural energies

THE EFFECTS OF GEOPATHIC STRESS

Like exposure to electromagnetic fields, spending long periods of time in areas prone to geopathic stress may undermine your immune system and cause you to suffer from ill health. This is because we are made up of energy ourselves, so any stimulus such as sound, vibration or EMFs will affect us in terms of resonance and the vibration of our own molecules. Our bodies vibrate in a certain way, and it is possible to influence this positively or negatively. (You will find more about this natural vibration in Part VI.) Our own electromagnetic force is balanced by a negative and positive polarity, just like a magnet. Geopathic stress may cause an unhealthy spiral in our own electromagnetic field, sucking waves of the same polarity and earthing them.

Because of this, geopathic stress is thought, in some cases, to contribute to cancer, chronic fatigue syndrome, MS, depression, anxiety, insomnia, and impair human growth hormones during sleep.

THE SYMPTOMS OF GEOPATHIC STRESS

There are some very obvious clues as to whether you may be suffering from geopathic stress. Use the following as a guide:

- Firstly, do you feel better when you leave your house for periods of time? Do you seem to recover your energy, well-being and sleep better if you stay somewhere else for a few days?

- Did you notice that illnesses, mishaps, or bad luck started to happen to you and your family when you moved in to your current home?

- Did the previous owner suffer with health problems?

- Has there been a high turnover in the number of people who have lived in your residence previously? This could indicate an 'unhealthy' house.

- Has anyone else commented that there is an 'atmosphere' in your home?

- Do you know of any underground streams, excavations or chemical works that might interfere with the energies of your home?

WHAT TO DO IN A CASE OF
GEOPATHIC STRESS

Most of this book focuses on self-help techniques. However, in the case of geopathic stress, if you think that your home or work place may be affected, then I suggest that you call in a good dowser. (See Resources for advice on whom to contact.) A dowser will use a variety of equipment to ascertain if you have problems with geopathic stress in your house. They may use metal dowsing rods (similar to those used by water diviners, namely two parallel rods, which cross when the dowser detects distorted electromagnetic fields), a liquid-filled compass, a pendant (a weighted object, suspended by a thread which, through gyrations, can show energy fields). They also use very sensitive electromagnetic test equipment such as a milli-Gauss meter, which can detect changes in the earth's magnetic field. As well as checking for geopathic stress, a good dowser will also advise you on electromagnetic stress caused by electrical equipment. As already explained, EMFs are made more powerful and are allegedly more harmful in the presence of geopathic stress.

A good dowser can pinpoint areas of geopathic stress such as underground streams, and may advise you to move your bed, or where you sit or work. A dowser may use crystals such as an amethyst to deflect certain geopathic stress or EMFs from the windows. Some dowsers also claim that mirrors can insulate and deflect the earth's energies. In extreme situations, if your house and environment are making you ill, a dowser may advise you to move. This is because, whatever treatments you undertake to try to restore your energy, the good work will all be undone whenever you spend time or sleep in an area of geopathic stress. You need to sort out your environment first, before proper healing can take place.

MY OWN STORY

My husband and I had quite an extraordinary experience in our last house, which leaves me in no doubt that geopathic stress can be a major factor in causing ill health and fatigue. In 1987 we moved to a very old cottage in East Sussex. At this point, we were both very healthy. Within two months, my husband became ill with pneumonia. This was followed by bouts of extreme anxiety and depression, from which he had never suffered before. Within a year, I was suffering from chronic insomnia, which was followed by extreme exhaustion, brain fog, anxiety and muscle aches. In 1990, I was diagnosed with ME (Chronic Fatigue Syndrome). Over the next three years I tried everything to get well, but I became weaker and weaker, and by 1993 was in a wheel-chair. I would spend long periods with my parents in Hampshire, where I always felt much better. Several people commented that they thought our house had a strange atmosphere and one guest claimed to have seen a ghost. (Some dowsers say that 'presences' can be caused by geopathic stress.)

One day we decided to get out a map. Our house was built on a hill, dated back to the fourteenth century, and had an old well in the garden (which may indicate an underground stream.) Lining up the churches, we were amazed to see that our house had five ley lines, which crossed through it! Ley lines are a network of energy lines that are believed to magnify and manipulate natural magnetic forces. Churches and standing stones are typically built along them. They can cause a healthy or unhealthy effect. For example, if ley lines cross, most dowsers consider that this may be detrimental to health. One or two might have been considered unusual, but to have so many was extraordinary. The map showed quite clearly that they intersected at our house, and not at the larger farmhouse next door.

We called in a feng shui master. He was accompanied by a Chinese lady who was an architect and was in the UK on sabbatical. (In the east, feng shui, which takes account of the earth's energies, is considered so important when designing and building, that it forms part of an architect's training.) They advised us to remove an internal wall, which faced the front door, and this we did. The house immediately felt better.

We then decided to ask the advice of Alf Riggs, (see Resources), a very famous international dowser who has been used in court cases to give evidence of illness caused by electromagnetic and geopathic stress. Riggs used various meters and a pendulum to analyse our problems. These included a geomagnetor to evaluate DC radiation, an instrument to measure AC fields, and a device that records gamma and X-ray activity. He discovered that we were sleeping above an underground stream and the negative effects of this were exacerbated by my husband's electric piano and midi-computer system, which was directly under the bed, in the room below. Riggs believes that the combination of underground water and an AC electromagnetic field (such as that caused by our computer and piano) is a major contributory factor in ME and Chronic Fatigue Syndrome. In addition to this, at least two of the ley lines running through the house were causing us problems. Riggs advised us to move the bed, and to move the piano to another area of the house. After this, I started to sleep better.

In 1995 we moved, and our health and circumstances changed dramatically for the better. Riggs visited our new cottage, and confirmed that all was well. Many of our visitors commented that the atmosphere of our new cottage was much better than that of the house in East Sussex. The previous resident lived here for 45 years – a good sign. The last we heard of our former home was that the people who bought the house from us, and who were very keen to live there for the rest of their lives, moved out after only three years. We don't know why.

I think the moral of this story is to listen to your instincts. I always felt that our last house was causing us to have ill health and bad luck, but my husband put this down to superstition on my part. It was only when he met Alf Riggs and saw the scientific evidence, that he was persuaded of the potential harm to health from geopathic stress and electromagnetic fields.

39

Help Yourself to the Earth's Natural Energy

The earth's natural electromagnetic frequency of about 7.8–8 Hertz per second is said to help to energise and heal, and is similar to the magnetic vibration put out by healers.

Travelling in metal containers like cars, aeroplanes and trains blocks out the earth's magnetic frequency, which is one reason why travelling can be so tiring. You can counteract this, and take advantage of our planet's natural healing energy, by walking barefoot whenever you can, especially on grass, earth or sand. Also, wear shoes with leather soles. They are less likely to block out the natural magnetic field than rubber or plastic.

The two exercises given here will help to put you in contact with the earth's magnetic frequencies by the physical effect of you making actual contact with the ground. The benefits of this are then enhanced by you visualising energy entering your system.

TREE EXERCISE ONE

Next time you are in the countryside, your garden or near a park, find a large tree. An oak tree or an ash tree is best as they have deep roots. Sit with your back to the tree, so that you have as much contact with your spine as possible. The bottom of your spine should be at the base of the tree, on the ground, with your legs in front of you. Close your eyes and slow your breathing down. As you breathe in, imagine that you are taking in energy from the tree. As you breathe out, imagine that any negative burdens you carry are being blown away in the air. Let sorrow, anger, despair, grief and disappointment all float away on your out-breath. Each time you breathe in, really visualise the energy you are taking in from the tree. You might like to imagine this as a colour or a sound, travelling up your spine to your head. Sit like this for at least 15 minutes.

TREE EXERCISE TWO

This is a very simple yoga balancing exercise. Stand upright on the grass, barefoot, with your feet hip-width apart. Check your posture. You should be evenly balanced over your feet, not too far forward nor too far back. Check that your pelvis is central by swinging it forwards and backwards, and then to the centre. Lift your breast-bone and relax your shoulders. Shift your weight onto your left side. Finally, check that your head is balanced on your neck, not pulled too far forward nor too far back. Now lift your right leg and tuck your right foot into your left inner thigh (see Diagram 4). Keep your right hip open by taking your knee out to the side. Take your hands into a prayer position in front of your chest. If your balance is secure, lift your hands up over your head. As you stand like this, imagine that you are a tree, with your roots reaching down into the earth, securing you and taking nutrients up into your body. Visualise your arms as being the branches of your tree, lifting up towards the sky, taking in nourishment from the sun. It will help your balance if you focus your gaze on a spot in front of you which you can concentrate on. When you have held the position comfortably for a few minutes, repeat on the other side, holding for the same amount of time as you held the pose before.

Diagram 4: The Tree

40

Energise Your Environment with Feng Shui

If you want more energy, it is very important that your whole environment reflects this – both at work and at home. Many converts to the ancient art of feng shui, which is based on harnessing natural 'chi', or energy from the earth, believe that those who apply it can live in peace and harmony with the planet. Within feng shui is the concept of natural energy lines. These are seen as dragon (masculine energy) and tiger (feminine energy), which cross the land and are used by the Chinese to harness optimum health and vitality wherever they build. They are similar to our idea of ley lines. Until recently, the Chinese did not excavate or mine the land, because they knew it could upset the earth's energies. The Chinese also ensure that buildings are not constructed in geopathically stressed areas.

Other factors influence the ancient art of feng shui. For example, straight lines are considered to cause bad chi, as energy can run away too quickly. A road with bends, therefore, would be considered a better position for a house. Likewise, stagnant rivers, burial grounds, sewage farms or rubbish dumps nearby to residential areas are considered bad, as they give off unhealthy chi. In this way, the eastern concept of feng shui and the scientific evidence of geopathic stress are linked.

Good feng shui means that chi, or energy, can move freely around the home, without being stuck in dark corners, or escaping through open spaces. Using feng shui tools such as light, mirrors and plants can make a huge difference to your environment.

Top Tips For Energising Your Home

Try the following to energise your home or work place:

- Aim to de-clutter anything that you don't use. An excess of possessions like clothes, ornaments and paperwork attracts bad energy. Always repair or throw out anything that is broken or needs repair. If you don't use it, bin it.

- Introduce as much light and air into your rooms as possible. Open windows at least twice a week to sweep in new energy. Put spotlights in dark corners and use mirrors to reflect light in passageways. Long, narrow corridors or cramped corners should be painted white and be well lit. This stops the energies of the room becoming stagnant. In this way you are enhancing the stale energy of a tight space.

- Houseplants give off extra oxygen and attract good energy. Throw out any dead or dying plants. Dried flowers are considered bad in feng shui, as they are said to attract negative energy.

- Protruding corners create 'knife edges', which are considered bad. Avoid sitting on or sleeping near furniture with sharp corners.

- Introduce harmonising colours into your living space to help calm or revitalise you. You will find more about colour therapy in Part VI; but in feng shui, cool colours like green or blue are used for bedrooms as they have a calming effect, whereas lively colours like yellow or red may be used in living areas such as the dining room.

- Overhead beams can cause bad energy. Hang a five-rod wind chime on any beam that you sit or sleep under.

- Pets create good feng shui as they help to move energy around.

- Make sure that your main front door doesn't open on to a cramped dark area. It shouldn't face a lavatory, a staircase or a mirror, as this will reflect the energy back out of the house. In feng shui, if the stairs lead down to your front door, or if you can see the back door from the front door, energy may drain from your home. You can prevent this by placing bushy plants outside, to stop the energy running away.

- Don't hang mirrors in your bedroom. They create too much energy and will prevent you from sleeping well. Likewise, don't sleep under a window. You shouldn't sleep with your feet facing the door. Your bedroom door shouldn't face a staircase, a mirror or another door. If it does, keep it closed, or hang a wind chime there. Never sleep facing away from the door. Cover bedroom windows with heavy drapes so that you are not over-stimulated by the energy of the morning light.

- Keep lavatory lids down at all times. Don't decorate your toilet with plants or flowers.

- Playing loud music in a room for at least ten minutes helps to move the energies of the room around.

- Don't have your cooker next to the sink or refrigerator. This creates a clash between water and fire elements.

- Avoid prickly plants like cacti. The spikes attract bad energy.

- Mops and brooms are associated with sweeping negative and stale energy away. Hide all materials when you have finished cleaning.

- Don't hang your washing out at night. It will absorb the energy of the night and upset your feng shui.

- Trim and deadhead your house plants regularly. Straggly, dried up or wilting plants are bad.

Some of these ideas may seem quite far-fetched, but there is a lot of evidence that feng shui works, so they are worth a try. Many major corporations use it and have improved their business significantly. The important thing to take from all this is that it is good for your health to pay attention to your environment. If you live and work in light, airy spaces that you find pleasing and want to actually *be* in, then this will uplift your spirits and have a positive effect on your health and energy.

PART VI

The Mind-Body-Spirit Solution to Your Energy Crisis

If you want true, sustaining vitality and a sense of purpose in your life, then you need a balance between mind, body *and* spirit. Most people pay attention to the first and second of these but not the third. So, this final section looks at ideas to help you to nurture your spirit as well as your physical body. Mind, body and spirit are all connected – you cannot have good health without paying attention to all three.

Most people understand what is meant by 'mind' and 'body'. But how do we define 'spirit'? To some people, getting in touch with their spiritual nature might mean thinking about the existence of God. Others are uncomfortable with the notion of God and, instead, like to call this a 'Universal Life Force', or a 'Power of Love' or 'Light' or 'Higher Power'.

Whatever the concept of spirit means to you, it does raise the question that there may be more to life than just material existence; that there must be something special and good that has the ability to unite us all, and give some direction and meaning to our lives. Working on your spiritual nature will enhance your sense of self-worth and self-esteem, which in turn will give you energy. This is because you will feel that you are nourished through love by something greater that is there to support you and to give you purpose for being.

This part of the book also looks at Universal Energy – the concept that there is an energy force all around you that you can learn how to control, store and direct via your own energy centres, to maximise your stamina.

41

Meditate for Mind, Body and Spirit!

One of the best things you can do, if you want more energy, is to meditate regularly. However, you may find it difficult to have the discipline to set aside 20 minutes every day, and you may not find it easy to meditate at first. This next section should convince you that it is worth investing your time, and will also give you some easy techniques to get you started.

Meditation gives you energy because you are giving your brain a huge rest from the incessant internal chattering that goes on all the time. It is said that 20 minutes of proper meditation is equivalent to four hours' sleep. One of the reasons for this is that when you meditate, your brain goes into the Alpha state, where your brain waves slow down. This is a very relaxed state where you are still just awake, but your brain waves are slower and calmer.

Meditation is about stopping, or learning to still your mind. It can be quite difficult to get the hang of this at first, but do persevere because the feeling of peace, calm and silence you will experience is truly wonderful and invigorating. Meditation is said to happen when everything stops, when you let your thoughts go, and notice the silence

between your breaths. This silence will also help you to con-
nect to your spiritual side. If you consider your thoughts, they
can be like a noisy pack of leashed dogs, always pulling you in
different directions. Another analogy is of the 'thought chain'.
One thought leads to another, then another, then another.
This is very tiring and can lead to mental fatigue. In fact, if you
think about it, an unruly mind may be at the root of your
tiredness. A mind crammed with the trivia of everyday things
may also stop you from finding your spiritual direction in life.
So, learning techniques that enable you to stop this mental
exhaustion will put you back in control again.

PREPARATION FOR MEDITATION

Find a quiet spot where you can sit quietly without
being disturbed. Sit comfortably with your spine straight.
Relax as much as possible; check that your shoulders are
not raised and that your jaw is not tense. You are aiming
to put all your cares and worries aside for 20 minutes.
This is easier said than done, but some of the mental
exercises below will help you. Remind yourself that this
is *your* time and that you don't need to think about
anything until you have finished. Try to close off your
senses. If you hear any outside noise, just accept it but
don't focus on the sound.

LEARNING TO CONCENTRATE

Learning to concentrate is very good preparation for
learning to meditate, as it helps to rein your mind in so that

it is not wandering along the 'thought chain'. If you find your mind drifting, just bring it gently back. Here are some ideas to help you focus.

1. Close your eyes. Look upwards at the space between your eyebrows. Now, start to slow your breathing down. Just follow your breath, counting to four slowly on your in-breath, and four on your out-breath.

2. Repeat the above exercise but leave a pause between your in-breath and your out-breath. Notice the silence and darkness in the space between your breaths.

3. A mantra can be a very useful aid to meditation. A classic yoga mantra, which you repeat silently, is 'Sa Ham'. (Sanskrit for 'I am that'.) Say Sa to yourself as you slowly breathe in and Ham as you breathe out. The Sa represents the sound of the hissing, sibilant in-breath. Ham represents the sighing sound of the out-breath. Focus on the sound of your breath. If your mind starts to drift, gently bring it back to the sound of your mantra.

4. You can make up your own mantra: 'I Breathe in Peace and Energy' is a good one to start with as it focuses your mind on a positive affirmation. Some people find it more helpful to concentrate on something visual. A flower is a good example. Put a single flower in a vase in front of you. Really look at the flower as you breathe slowly in and out. Notice its texture and detail. Now, close your eyes and imagine the flower in your mind's eye. Open your eyes again and continue concentrating on the flower.

Meditate To Beat Fatigue

You should practise one of the above exercises every day for a few weeks. Once you feel that you are learning to discipline your mind and that you are able to sit quietly without your mind chasing away in all directions, you can start to practise the following meditation to beat fatigue:

• Sit quietly as before, with your spine straight and your eyes closed.

• Aim to clear your mind of all its clutter and constant chatter. It might help to see your mind as a pond with ripples that slowly gets calmer so that the surface is utterly still. Or you may like to imagine that you are looking at a blank screen in a cinema: you are really *looking* into the stillness and peace.

• If your mind starts to wander, take it back to watching your breath.

• Sit like this, trying to let everything go into stillness for at least 20 minutes.

If you can make the time and discipline to meditate every day, you *will* notice huge benefits. You will become calmer, find it more easy to cope in times of crisis, you will slow down your production of stress-related chemicals and you will discover spiritual growth. Best of all is that you will notice a huge increase in your health and energy.

42

Visualisations

If you find meditation difficult, you may like to use visualisations, which have a similar effect of slowing and calming the brain down. Visualisations (where you close your eyes and imagine a scenario) are a very useful way of increasing your energy levels and training your mind into a more positive, effective framework. You can use visualisations to make what you want to happen, *really* happen. Visualisations work rather like self-hypnosis. You relax and calm your mind, which allows your subconscious to become more susceptible to positive suggestions. For example, if you visualise a scenario where you are healthy and energetic, you are training your mind to make this become true.

POSITIVE VISUALISATIONS

Here are some visualisations incorporating affirmations that are very powerful. You may like to record them on to a tape or get a friend to read them out to you.

The magic garden

Lie down, relax and make yourself comfortable. Imagine that you are floating on a cloud, which is very soft and very cosy. Above you, the sun is shining brightly. Feel it on your face. Feel it warming the whole of your body, which is bathed in a golden glow. Now imagine this golden colour being centred at your navel so that it is radiating warmth and light to every cell in your body. As you inhale, feel that you are breathing in energy. As you breathe out, let all tension and tiredness float away from you.

Now, you look up and see a golden ladder, climbing into the sky, towards the light. Get up from your cloud and climb the ladder. Each step you take makes you feel more and more revitalised. At the top of the ladder is a door. You open the door and find that you are in a beautiful garden. Take some time to walk around the garden, where you see your favourite flowers and plants. This is a special place, so really imagine what your perfect garden looks like. Smell the scent of the flowers and hear the birds singing. What flowers do you see? Do you see any animals? In this magic garden, all your problems are left behind and you have perfect health. As you walk around your garden you come across a bench with big, soft cushions, by a stream. Sit down on the bench and relax, letting the sound of the crystal clear waters wash over you. You feel very safe. Just enjoy being here, with all your problems so far away that they seem insignificant for now, so that you can enjoy your perfect health.

After a few minutes of relaxation, you decide to get up and follow the stream. As you do so, it takes you through a beautiful forest. Notice the tall trees and smell the sharp scent of pine needles. The trees make you feel warm and protected.

The stream now takes you up a steep hill. You climb to the top of the hill, where you come across a waterfall. By the waterfall is a hand mirror. Pick up the mirror. Take time now, to look into the mirror and see yourself as you would like to be; healthy, happy and full of energy. Really notice what you look like and accept that this person *is* you. As you gaze, repeat the following affirmation three times: 'I am calm, I have endless energy from the Universe, I am renewed'.

Now turn around, go back down the hill, into the forest and back into the garden. Go back through the door. You are now going to climb down the ladder. Each step you take leaves you feeling relaxed and refreshed. Step back down, into your cloud. Notice that the sky around you is shot through with the beautiful, iridescent colours of a gorgeous sunset. As you lie back on your cloud you acknowledge that your beautiful garden is always there for you, whenever you want to feel peaceful and revitalised. All you have to do is to close your eyes and imagine it.

Count to five and open your eyes. Rub your hands together and have a few stretches.

LETTING GO OF HEAVY BURDEN

Close your eyes and relax. See yourself on the bank of a fast-flowing river. Hear the rushing sound the water makes. Smell the fresh, open air. Now think about any negative feelings that you have. Imagine these as streamers, flowing out of your navel. For example, you might see anger, guilt, disappointment, hurt, or you might see a relationship you need to let go of. Now imagine that you are picking up something from the river bank to cut the streamers away from you. It might be a pair of golden scissors. Or perhaps you need something more robust like a pair of garden shears. Or, if your negative streamers are very tough – you may even visualise a machete or chainsaw! You are now going to cut your negative streamers away from you. As you do, they start to float across the river, into the sun. The breeze helps them to blow across. As you watch, they disappear into the light, leaving you feeling happy and energised as your heavy burdens are removed. Now, repeat the following five times: 'I clear and remove any negative energy, which leaves me light and revitalised'.

The ball of light

Try this next visualisation twice a week to keep your energy levels from dropping. Lie on your back, somewhere comfortable. Relax and close your eyes. Imagine a ball of white healing light above the top of your head and at the soles of your feet. As you breathe in, feel light coming up through your feet, up through your spine, and revitalising your whole body, until it meets the ball of white light at the top of your head. As you breathe out, picture moving the light from the top of your body back to your feet. As it passes through your navel, it turns to bright sunshine yellow and when it gets to your feet it turns to red. Repeat this for at least ten minutes. Now say to yourself: 'I ask the Universal Life Force to raise my energy levels'. Repeat this three times. Now slowly open your eyes, rub your hands together and have a good stretch.

Try to use one affirmation that you repeat several times a day. Use any of the visualisations from this chapter whenever you want to feel calm and refreshed, or make up your own to suit your particular situation.

THE POWER OF AFFIRMATIONS

An affirmation (an uplifting word or phrase) is very beneficial and, if used everyday, can help to energise your whole system. Like visualisations, affirmations work because if you tell yourself something often enough, you will start to believe it and make it happen. Think back to when you were a child. If a teacher told you that you were stupid often enough, you eventually believed it. Likewise, if you were told something positive, like you were clever, or beautiful, that also became true for you. Affirmations work because, when you repeat a phrase often enough, you train your subconscious into taking a new direction,

To make an affirmation, you need to give yourself a simple, one-line goal. Now all you do is to repeat this to yourself or out loud. Your affirmation should always be positive and in the present tense. For example, saying 'I would like to be healthy. I will have energy' will not be as powerful as saying 'I am healthy. I have energy'. Believe that your affirmation will come true. Picture yourself as you will be – happy and healthy, confident, successful – or whatever your desired outcome is. You may even like to write it down and pin it up somewhere to remind you of your goal.

Some Suggested Affirmations

- I have full health.

- I am full of energy and vitality.

- I am calm and peaceful.

- I am confident and successful.

- I am happy and content with my life.

AFFIRMATIONS WITH MOVEMENT

The following exercise is a very beneficial way of incorporating an energy-boosting exercise with a sequence of positive affirmations. The movement helps to crystallise the effect of the affirmations. You can do this at home and say the words silently to yourself if you like, although the sequence is more powerful if you can say the words out loud:

- Stand upright, with your hands stretched out horizontally. Increase this stretch by imagining that you are pushing the walls away with your hands. Say: 'I am healthy'.

- Next, bend your knees and bend your elbows, with your hands pointing upwards. Say: 'I have stamina'.

- Next, stretch your arms up to the sky and come up on to your toes, so that you are really stretching upwards. Say: 'I have energy'.

- Come down from your toes and wrap your arms around yourself, so that you are hugging yourself. Now say: 'I am centred and calm'.

- Finally, circle your arms over your head and down by your sides like a windmill. Say: 'The Universe gives me Endless Energy'.

43

Tap in to the Universal Energy Force

Wouldn't it be amazing if there were energy all around you – a Universal Energy Force, which you could tap into to recharge your batteries whenever you felt tired? It would be like a giant mains electricity generator, rather than the small power pack that you carry with you, constantly available for you to access whenever you need revitalising.

This energy *does* exist and, by using quite simple techniques, you can learn to store, control and direct this energy. This may sound difficult to accept. Nevertheless, scientific evidence (through quantum physics) shows that the universe consists of patterns of energy, of which atoms are a part. In other words, everything, including you, has a vibration or energy force. We each have an electromagnetic field and other vibrations can affect this field, and this is well known by those who study eastern philosophy and yoga.

You will know the feeling if you meet someone whose energy field clashes with yours – you feel as if they have a bad feeling or 'vibration'. Conversely, you may find that some people actually *give* you more energy. All that is happening is that you are tuning into your own energy field – and picking up on their energy.

In yoga, this Universal Energy is called Prana. Those who practise yoga regularly and who meditate can begin to learn how to maximise this Universal Energy flow. Prana is said to be the sum of all the energy in the universe and to consist of, among other things, electromagnetic forces, gravity, oxygen and positive and negative ions.

It is said that if you can learn to access this Universal Energy Force, then you have the key to perfect mental and physical health. Our bodies are saturated with Universal Energy, but our health depends upon how we store and use it. Sometimes this energy gets blocked through ill health, emotions, stress or poor diet. When your own energy is not flowing properly, you become ill because Universal Energy can't flow properly through your body.

ACCESSING UNIVERSAL ENERGY

You can access Universal Energy through:

1. The *air* you breathe and the way in which you breathe (see Chapter 44)

2. *Sunshine* (Chapter 45)

3. *Food* (Chapter 46)

4. By keeping your *energy centres* (chakras) in good health (see Chapter 47).

Accepting and understanding the idea of Universal Energy may encourage you to make simple adjustments to your diet, and be aware of how the power of fresh air and sunshine can make a real difference to your own energy levels.

The next three chapters look at sunshine, air and food, and their relation to Universal Energy in more detail. Chapter 47 explains your Energy Centres and suggests how you can use them to access the never-ending supply of Universal Energy.

44

The Power of the Air

To maximise the power of the Universal Energy force through using air, you need to be aware of your breathing, and to keep it slow and rhythmic. Any of the breathing exercises already given in this book (for example see Chapter 6) will help you to maximise your energy levels.

Breathing in fresh air is always best, but if this is not possible, you could consider investing in an ioniser, which converts the air into negative ions. An air ion is a molecule that has gained or lost an electron. Negative ions, which are very beneficial for health, are a molecule of oxygen *with* an electron. Positive ions, which can lead to ill health, are attracted to electromagnetic fields, such as are found in offices, near computers or even by power lines. (Static electricity attracts dust, which converts ions to become positive.) Some scientists believe that the damage from exposure to electromagnetic fields is partly because of the presence of positive ions, which causes the blood to flow more slowly. At a full moon, because of the magnetic changes to the earth, and just before a thunderstorm, the air is full of positive ions, which can cause some people to have aches or pains, or to feel that the air is 'heavy'. Other symptoms from positive ions include headaches, anxiety, lack of concentration and fatigue. Certain winds, such as the Mistral in France, are known to cause health problems including feelings of irritability, depression and fatigue. This is because these winds are full of positive ions from dust and sand. Pollution, dust and smoke all attract positive ions and for this reason, should be avoided wherever possible.

Negative ions are created in nature by sunlight, wind, waterfalls, surf and rain. After a thunderstorm, the air is recharged with negative ions and feels fresh and clean. This is a good time to open a window and breathe in deeply! Universal Energy is highest in areas where there are many negative ions, such as near the sea or in mountain regions. Studies have shown that wounds heal quicker in areas charged with negative ions.

TIPS FOR HARNESSING THE POWER OF AIR

The following tips will help you to take advantage of one of the major forces of Universal Energy:

- Open a window whenever possible. Sleep with the window ajar. In feng shui, the Chinese believe that fresh air energises the whole house, bringing in 'chi' or positive energy.

- Try to take a walk in the fresh air once a day.

- Use an ioniser where you work, particularly if you work with a computer, which causes positive ions. Ionisers can dramatically reduce harmful airborne particles including viruses, bacteria, pollen dust and smoke. Additionally, they can increase vitality and result in a feeling of well-being.

- Breathe in fresh air deeply and slowly to revitalise and recharge your whole system. Close your eyes, breathe in slowly for a count of four, hold for two, then exhale slowly for a count of four. Repeat three more times.

- Smoke, dust and pollution are the enemies of Universal Energy. Whenever possible, try to avoid stale air as it will deplete your vitality. Breathe in fresh air whenever you can.

EXERCISE TO MAXIMISE THE POWER OF AIR

- Open the window, then sit in a chair, with your spine upright, or lie on the bed. Slow your breathing down. Notice the difference between your in-breath and out-breath. You are now going to start to count, using a technique that helps to balance and restore energy, using your breath. You will be using your mind to *visualise* the alternate nostril breath described in Chapter 6.

- As you count one, imagine that you are breathing in only through your right nostril. Count one again, and visualise breathing out of your left nostril. Now count two and breathe in through your left nostril, and count two as you breathe out of your right nostril. Count three and visualise energy and breath flowing through your right nostril, then breathe out for the count of three again, this time through your left nostril. Count four, breathe in through your left nostril, and count four as you breathe out through your right nostril. On the count of five breathe in through both nostrils, and count five as you breathe out through both nostrils. For the count of six, breathe in through your right nostril and count six again as you breathe out through your left nostril.

- Continue in this way, using your imagination to visualise breathing through alternate nostrils, but using both nostrils each time you reach a multiple of five such as 10, 15, 20, 25 and so on. Each time you forget to count, go back to number one. See if you can reach 100 breathing in fresh air like this.

45

Sunshine, the Energy Generator

If a plant lacks sunshine, it will begin to wilt and will eventually die. Like water, you need a certain amount of sunshine for energy. In eastern philosophy, sunshine is also known as one of the main sources of Universal Energy. This isn't as odd as it sounds – everyone feels better when the sun shines. However, you actually need to go outside and sit in the sun to take in some of the benefits of solar energy. Ideally, you should go outside and be exposed to the sun for at least an hour a day. However, this isn't always possible.

Many people in the northern hemisphere suffer from SAD (seasonal affective disorder) during the winter months. Symptoms include depression and lack of energy. Sunlight is measured in lux (a unit of light). Inside, in the northern hemisphere in the winter, the light is around 1,000 lux. Being by the sea on a sunny day in the Mediterranean region is around 2,500 lux. Light is made up of various wave-forms, including ultraviolet A, B and C rays and infrared rays. If you think you might suffer from

SAD and you notice that your energy levels dip considerably during the winter, you may like to consider investing in a light box, which will supply you with this full spectrum of light that you are missing. (See Resources for more details.)

Our hormones are profoundly affected by light. In the morning, for example, the pineal gland starts to produce cortisol as it gets lighter. Likewise, the hormone associated with sleep, melatonin, is produced as it starts to get dark. In the old days, our ancestors worked very much with the rhythms of the earth. They went to bed when it got dark and got up when it was light, whatever the season. In this way, they worked with natural light and natural rhythms.

Research shows that you benefit *more* from sunshine if you don't protect your eyes with sunglasses or your skin with sunblock. The sun can then help you to process vital nutrients such as vitamin D. However, make sure never to look directly at the sun. Like everything, the sun should be enjoyed in moderation.

SUNSHINE VISUALISATION

You can benefit from light even in the winter by trying the following:

- Lie down on your bed or on the floor and relax. Let everything feel heavy. Close your eyes and slow down your breathing.

- Imagine you are lying on a beach. You can feel the hot sun warming your face and the rest of your body. In the distance, you hear the sea lapping against the shore.

Tune the sound of the sea into the sound of your breathing so that the sea ebbs and flows in tune with your breath. Smell the sea and the perfume of your suntan lotion. Really try to capture the smells and sounds. Add to them if you want.

• Feel yourself getting warmer and warmer as the heat radiates out to every cell in your system, bringing healing energy. Really imagine the feeling of lying in warm sunshine.

Psychologists say that the brain reacts in the same way to fantasy as it can to reality. In other words, if you can visualise the sun strongly enough, your body will get some of the physiological benefits that you would have if you really were lying in the sun.

46

Food as Your Energy Fuel

Food is the third way in which you take in Prana, or Universal Energy. All the ideas described in this book will help to boost your energy but as we saw in Part III, one of the most important things to consider, if you really want to beat fatigue, is to make sure that you are eating a good diet. Eating poor quality junk food is one of the main causes of tiredness. Think about it: if you were going to collect wood from a forest to make a fire and you chose the fastest method, collecting small dry twigs, then you would have a fire that burns brightly, but soon dies. If you took a bit more time, and collected bigger, more seasoned wood, then your fire might not burst into bright flames at the beginning but would make a good, warm fire, which would last. In the same way, if you eat lots of sugary snacks and use alcohol and caffeine to give you instant energy you will have a quick lift, but you will feel very tired soon after. You need good quality food, like good quality wood for your fire, to give you enduring stamina. Follow the tips on nutrition in Part III and you should then be well on your way to increasing your energy.

Tap Into The Universal Energy Force Through Your Diet

Here are some reminders to help you increase your intake of energy-giving foods:

- Eat plenty of fresh, whole grains, together with plenty of fruit and vegetables.

- Always eat organic food if possible.

- Add some protein to your diet such as fish, free-range chicken, nuts, eggs or plain, live yoghurt, together with complex carbohydrates and essential fats such as butter, olive oil or milk.

- Drink at least 2 litres (3.5 pt) of water a day.

- Don't drink water when you eat. You need certain enzymes to digest your food so that you get maximum energy from your diet. Water dilutes these essential enzymes. Drink water between meals instead.

- Avoid processed or junk food. This includes food that contains sugar or additives.

- Eat regular meals to keep your blood sugar levels stable. Always eat breakfast.

- Always remember to eat slowly and chew your food thoroughly so that you can utilise and assimilate all the nutrients in your food.

47

Vitalise Your Energy Centres

As we have already seen, everything in the Universe has a vibration or energy force, which you can use to increase your own vitality. You are an energy being yourself, and you vibrate at a certain frequency. Indeed, your electromagnetic force, or aura, can be seen using Kirlian photography, a form of photography invented in Russia that shows the electromagnetic activity of a body as a luminescence. Universal Energy is taken in to your body via your Energy Centres. These are also known as chakras, which is an ancient Sanskrit word meaning a whirl, or wheel of energy. So, each of your Energy Centres is like a spinning vortex of vitality that takes in nourishment from the universe. You can learn how to raise the vibration of your own energy, by understanding how your Energy Centres take in Prana, or Universal Energy.

There are many ways to work on your Energy Centres, so that you can take advantage of and maximise this universal vitality. For example, certain crystals, which vibrate at the relevant frequency, can be used to balance them. So can homeopathy, Bach flower remedies and essential oils, which also have a vibrational note. Visualisations, working with colour, music, chanting and mantras, will also help to bring maximum Universal Energy to your Energy Centres. You will learn more on how to use these in the following chapters.

THE SEVEN ENERGY CENTRES

You have seven main Energy Centres, which run parallel with your spine. First is your Root Energy Centre, which is situated at the base of your spine, and points down to take up energy from the earth. It is associated with your adrenal, reproductive and bowel systems. On an emotional level it relates to feelings of being grounded in the here and now. Next is your Sacral Energy Centre, situated around your pubic area. It relates to your reproductive system, bladder and kidneys. Emotionally this chakra is associated with sensuality and relationships with others. Then comes your Solar Plexus Energy Centre, which is near your navel. I look at this chakra in detail in the next chapter as it is most associated with your energy. Next is the Heart Energy Centre which is associated with your heart, lungs and thymus gland. It relates to the feelings of love, empathy, forgiveness and compassion. Your Throat Energy Centre relates to your voice, ears, thyroid gland and endocrine system, as well as the lungs. This chakra is associated with communication. Your Brow Energy Centre and Crown Energy Centre are both associated with your brain and intellectual functions, as well as your spiritual state (see Diagram 5).

Each of your Energy Centres vibrates at a particular frequency and relates to a different aspect of your physical, emotional and spiritual health. Each one also relates to the vibration of a colour. For example, in the colour spectrum, red vibrates at a lower frequency than green, so therefore red relates to the lowest of your Energy Centres, the Root chakra. Green relates to your Heart Energy Centre, which is, of course, higher up. The vibration rate increases as you go further up towards the Crown Energy Centre. Your lower Energy Centres relate to your more earth-bound emotional and physical states and the higher ones to your brain and mind; and your spiritual direction. The first four Energy Centres also relate to the elements of earth, water, fire and air.

For your Energy Centres to function properly, so that they can take in maximum vitality, they need to be balanced. That means that they should not be too closed; or too open. Blocked or unbalanced Energy Centres can eventually lead to ill health and lack of energy. For instance, at the emotional level, your Solar Plexus Energy Centre relates to your ego and how you interact with other people. If your Solar Plexus Energy Centre is too closed, you may be greedy, selfish and opinionated, whereas if your Solar Plexus Energy Centre is too open, you may depend on the approval of other people too much, without considering your own needs. If, however, this Energy Centre is balanced, you will be confident and centred without being self-centred and you will find it easy to relate well to those around you.

Each of your Energy Centres will guide you to what needs attention in your life. For example, the physical sensation of a headache, a stomach ache or a sore throat may indicate that the chakra relating to that particular area needs some work from you in order to help with energising that particular centre. Balancing your Energy Centres will give you much more vitality. They are all important, but in the next chapter I will focus on the Solar Plexus Energy Centre as this is particularly concerned with beating fatigue.

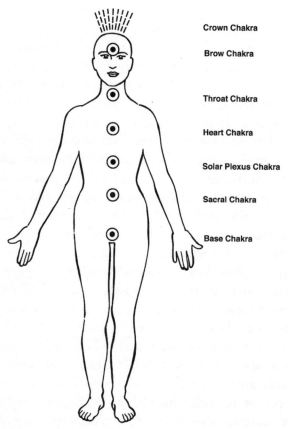

Crown Chakra

Brow Chakra

Throat Chakra

Heart Chakra

Solar Plexus Chakra

Sacral Chakra

Base Chakra

Diagram 5: The Chakras

48

Revitalising Your Solar Plexus Energy Centre

The Solar Plexus Energy Centre is situated around your navel area. It is represented by the colour yellow and the element of fire. It relates to your digestive system, your pancreas, stomach, liver, gall bladder, spleen and your small intestine. As previously explained, all your Energy Centres are important and need to be in balance, but this is perhaps the one that is the most vital for energy. This is because, as your 'Sun Centre', it relates to how you take in stamina and burn energy through your food. It is also important because it is about your sense of identity and your emotional relationships. It relates to who you actually *are* in relation to those around you.

As one of your major emotional centres, it is very much about your own identity. If this centre is too closed, then you may find it difficult to relate to other people or to make friends easily. Others may perceive you as cold, hostile or shy. Lack of motivation or willpower, the inability to project your personality in the world, not knowing who you really are, stress, depression and exhaustion may be a clue that your Solar Plexus Energy Centre is closed.

Conversely, if your Solar Plexus Centre is too open, you may be over-emotional, feeling intensely happy or sad, without ever feeling calm and centred. You may also find that you are over-reliant on other people's opinions, rather than considering your own path in life. You may also be susceptible to picking up the negative energies of others, which means you are using this Energy Centre rather like an unhealthy antenna to pick up on the emotional desires of those around you, rather than focusing on your own needs. If you live your life through other people's experiences and dramas and don't have clear boundaries, or if you think that you are ever too emotional or, on the other hand, too controlling, then you may need to do more work on your Solar Plexus Energy Centre.

If your Solar Plexus Energy Centre is balanced, then you will be confident in who you are, with clear boundaries, without being self-centred. You will be able to make healthy relationships and be able to deal successfully with others, while still being your own person. You will also be able to externalise your own emotions in an appropriate manner. Remember, although you need to be able to experience your feelings, you should have control over your emotions; they shouldn't control you.

If you give in too easily to other people's desires and wishes, or find it difficult to say 'no', or if you ever have tension or a feeling of 'butterflies in your tummy' try the following exercises to strengthen this chakra.

HOW TO HELP YOUR SOLAR PLEXUS ENERGY CENTRE

Simple tricks

If you feel that other people can drain you or suck away at your energy, imagine a mirror placed between you and them so that any negative energy they give out is not absorbed by you, but reflected back to them. Another trick is to fold your arms around your navel, thus placing a physical protective barrier between your own energies and theirs.

Visualisation

1. Lie on the floor and relax. Now breathe out slowly from your rib-cage area, using your diaphragm. Visualise the sun warming your navel area. Now imagine that the warm, golden light has moved into your Solar Plexus Energy Centre. Each time you breathe in, feel that you are breathing in energy and vitality, which emanate warmth and light to the rest of your body. Think of your body as a wheel, with the sun in the centre. Each out-breath pushes the warmth and energy further and further out to the rim of your wheel, so that your whole body is bathed in warmth and vitality. Lie quietly for a few minutes, enjoying the experience of warmth from your centre.

2. Now, each time you breathe out, see white light streaming from your nostrils. This white light is

going to encircle you in a protective cocoon. First, each out-breath pushes white light from your head down to your toes. Then the light moves under your feet, up your legs and back, to the top of your head and back down your front again. Each out-breath makes the circle of light stronger and stronger. Take a few minutes to feel safe and protected in your golden cocoon. Say the following affirmation twice: 'I am centred, I am healthy, I have energy'.

49

RECHARGE WITH COLOUR

You can use colour to help to increase your energy levels and also to balance your Energy Centres. This is because colour, like sound and light, *is* actual energy. By that I mean that each colour has its own vibration level in the colour spectrum. Red, for example, vibrates at a lower frequency than blue. This is why some blind people can learn to read colours – they can literally *feel* the different vibrations they give off.

Because each of your Energy Centres has its own relevant colour, you can actually help to balance your Energy Centres and the way you feel by what you wear, the colours in your home or office and by what lighting you use. For example, red will help your Root Energy Centre; it will help to ground you so that you feel as if you are connected to the world. Orange, which relates to your Sacral Energy Centre, can help to recharge your sexual energies. Yellow, for your Sun Energy Centre, can help you in your relationships with others, while staying centred in yourself. Green for your Heart Energy Centre is brilliant for opening up your heart to love. Wear light blue, particularly as a scarf around your throat, if you want help in being an effective communicator. This relates to your Throat Energy Centre. Indigo and violet or purple are closely aligned to your spiritual progress; they are the colours for the Brow and Crown Energy Centres. This is possibly why bishops wear purple: it is related to higher energies.

Translating this for every day you might choose red, orange and yellow to wear if you are feeling exhausted. However, be careful as these colours can be over-stimulating if you use them too much. Fast-food restaurants use these colours because their research shows that it makes people eat more food and more quickly! Even staff in hospitals in the UK have realised that colours have an effect on emotions and are now decorating their waiting rooms in green and blue to help people stay calm. I have decorated my own bedroom with blue, because I find it a peaceful colour, which helps me to relax. I like to wear a lot of red during the day, because I find it an uplifting colour, which gives me an energy boost.

CHOOSING COLOURS FOR ENERGY AND HEALTH

If you want to improve your own energy and health follow these basic guidelines when choosing colours:

- Red, orange and yellow are all energising colours. Wear them on the days you feel you need an extra lift.

- Green is excellent for depression. Nature is green, which

has a therapeutic effect on all of us, calming our emotions and lifting our spirit.

- Use blue if you want to feel tranquil; for example if your mind is racing with thoughts and ideas that you would like to slow down.

- Violet is also a calming colour, good to use if you feel hyperactive, or over-stimulated.

- Wear the colour that matches your Energy Centre as near to the relevant area as possible. For example, you could wear red trousers or a red skirt, as that is near your Root Energy Centre. A green shirt would be ideal for your Heart Energy Centre.

- Sunlight contains the full colour spectrum and is a direct source of energy. Remember to maximise your vitality by enjoying the sunshine, in moderation, whenever you can.

- Colour therapy works more effectively when it is used as a light source, so consider placing coloured bulbs in your living and work areas that relate to the mood you would like enhanced. Red lighting, for example, is too energising in a bedroom but light blue can work well if used carefully, remembering that too much can make a room cold. Light pink can be good to add to a living area.

- Try to avoid fluorescent lighting. This has very little of the colour spectrum, which is thought to be one of the contributing factors in Sick Building Syndrome at work (see Chapter 17). Full spectrum lighting or halogen lights are better as they have more of the light range found in sunlight and will actually make you feel more alert. They are used in commercial greenhouses to make plants grow, so you can imagine the positive effect such lighting will have on you!

50

Revitalise with Sound

Sound waves, like colour, are also energising. Because sound *is* energy (or vibration), if you use it in the right way, you can use it to beat fatigue and generally to boost your health. We all vibrate in different ways, which is why a range of sounds can affect our energy levels and mood differently. Like colour, each of your Energy Centres relates to a different sound. This all makes complete sense if you think about the way that music can affect you. For example, illness may be associated with tensions in certain parts of your body. Listening to certain music can help to relieve this. This works because certain harmonies relate to each of your Energy Centres.

DIFFERENT MUSIC FOR EACH ENERGY CENTRE

Playing Beethoven, for instance, may help digestive complaints. This relates to your Solar Plexus Energy Centre. Heart and lung disorders may respond to soaring music such as Vaughan Williams's *The Lark Ascending* (your Heart Energy Centre). Headaches (your Brow Energy Centre) may respond to Samuel Barber's *Adagio for Strings* or to plainsong chanting, which can lift you into an almost spiritual state as you become at one with the music.

It is easy to work out which music can help which of your Energy Centres. For most people, drum and dance music are very grounding as they help the Root Energy Centre. Sensual, soul music is generally good for the Sacral Energy Centre. Tchaikovsky is an emotional composer, so is good for opening the Solar Plexus and Heart Energy Centres. You may well feel the vibration in these areas if you play his music. However, if these centres are too open, you may not feel comfortable with such music, as it may overwhelm you and make you feel too emotional and tearful. Choral music can help your higher Energy Centres, try Handel's *Messiah* or listen to Gregorian chants, which have a similar effect to meditation and can slow down the brain waves, producing the more calming Alpha waves.

My husband teaches children with behavioural difficulties and often plays classical music when he is teaching. He finds it helps to calm down his students and aids their concentration. There is scientific evidence for this. Professor Jenkins, writing in the *Journal of the Royal Society of Medicine*, describes how the sound waves in the music of Mozart and Bach can actually boost children's IQ. Listening to these composers has been shown to increase spatial reasoning power, hand-eye co-ordination and other visual activities. In other words, some music really *does* energise the brain! In another study, epileptics were shown to experience a decrease in brain patterns that produce seizures after participants listened to Mozart's Sonata K448.

Classical music has actually been shown to lower blood pressure, body temperature and breathing patterns. In the case of heavy rock music, this has the opposite effect, so use your own instinct to play music that either energises or soothes you. What works for one person will not suit someone else.

So, think about how sound affects you, such as music, nature, birds singing, or even the traffic noise of a city or busy road. It can help to calm you, make you happy, inspired, emotional, romantic, or it can irritate you and make you angry. Some music (or certain vibrations) may actually make you feel *more* tired: I find House or heavy rock music confusing and tiring. Some modern music is aggressive and, when combined with strobe lighting, it can churn up all your Energy Centres, causing you to feel angry or disturbed. On the other hand, some modern music can be very positive, for example dance music may affect you in such a way that it actually gives you energy so that you *have* to move or dance to it! I have a friend with ME who swears by Van Morrison to make her feel better! I find that if I am having a nap during the day, the sound of mowing or vacuuming relaxes me and sends me to sleep. (And that's not just because someone else is doing the work!)

So, try to find the sound that appeals to you, whether it be wind chimes, Pavarotti or heavy rock. Whatever calms you when you need soothing, or energises you when you need a boost, just try the relevant music whenever you need some healing.

51

Chanting for Energy

Sound, as we saw in the last chapter, can be used for healing. Vibration (or sound) *is* energy and underlines everything in the universe. Even the earth has a vibration, around 7.8–8 Hertz, or cycles per second. This vibration is known as the Schumann Waves, after Professor W. Schumann discovered them in 1952. It is said that without this vibration, everything on the planet would eventually die. We have already seen how scientists who have measured brainwave patterns put out by healers have found that their brains emit a certain frequency during a healing session. It has also been discovered that the vibration of a cat's purr creates a natural healing process, and that cats who are wounded purr because it helps their bones and organs to grow stronger. Scientists from the Fauna Communications Research Institute in North Carolina in the US have found that between 27 and 44 Hertz is the frequency given by a cat's purr. Exposure to similar sound frequencies of between 20–50 Hertz has been shown to improve bone density in humans.

Because sound *is* energy, each word we use also has its own power. For example, all religions have mantras, powerful words whose vibrational tone has an effect. Think of 'Amen' and 'Hallelujah'. It is believed that repeating a mantra can transform, stabilise, purify, energise and focus us. Chanting and mantras are said to open our hearts and make love flow as well as purifying the atmosphere around us.

You can use mantras and chanting to help re-energise your Energy Centres. Here are two simple chanting exercises using a mantra (a short word or phrase) to help invigorate you. The first, *Om*, also known as *Aum*, is one of the classic and best mantras to start with. It is said to incorporate all the vibration of the universe and is traditionally used in eastern philosophy to help balance and invigorate all the Energy Centres. If practised every day, it can help you tune in to your real self, thereby bringing about quite profound changes. It is also very relaxing. Yoga teachers say that it brings about healing and energy by the vibration stimulating the nerve endings, which helps to energise the whole system. The second, *Om mane padme hum* (pronounced 'om manay padmay whom'), is a classic yoga chant, which also helps to stabilise, energise and heal.

Two Simple Mantras

1. Om

First, sit upright in a place where you will not be disturbed. You are going to make a lot of noise, so you don't want to be interrupted! Close your eyes, breathe in deeply from your diaphragm, open your mouth as wide as you can and, as you breathe out, sing '*ahhh*' (as you do if a doctor is looking down your throat). Using the same out-breath, start to bring your mouth into an '*o*' shape so that the sound becomes '*ooohh*'. Finally, still breathing out, bring your lips together so for the final part of the breath you are humming '*mmm*'. The sound should move from the back of your throat to the front of your mouth. When you put the sequence together on one out-breath, you should be humming a '*ah-oo-mm*' sound (*om*). Take a deep breath in and repeat at least five times. When you have finished, let the silence wash over you, keeping your eyes closed for a couple more minutes. As you practise the *Om* breath, you should aim to immerse yourself in the vibration; try and close off your mind so that you are not thinking of anything other than the sound.

2. Om mane padme hum

This time you are not going to hum, but rather repeat a very powerful phrase either out loud, or silently to yourself. '*Om mane padme hum*' is a Sanskrit phrase, which literally translated means 'The jewel in the heart of the lotus'. It is believed that many of the mantras in Sanskrit have a power just from their sound, and this particular one is said to be very good for lifting the spirits and for depression. Simply close your eyes, sit comfortably, and repeat the phrase slowly to yourself for five to ten minutes. Try and immerse yourself in the sound of the mantra. If your mind wanders, gently bring it back to the sound of '*Om mane padme hum*'.

52

Summary – Your Vitality Plan for Endless Energy

So, now you have the complete picture – everything you need to know to increase and maximise your energy levels. Before looking at your daily Energy Plan, here is a reminder of some quick energy boosts, useful whenever you need an extra burst of vitality.

INSTANT ENERGY BOOSTS

- Eat something nutritious like a handful of nuts or seeds and drink some water.

- Do an inverted posture, such as the Shoulder Stand. This will instantly revive you, as it takes fresh blood and nutrients to your head.

- Do the Alternate Nostril Breath for three minutes – it is a brilliant pick-me-up!

- Remember the cross-crawl? Simply get down on your

hands and knees and crawl round the room, using opposite limbs. If you would rather, you can march on the spot, lifting your legs high. This rebalances your brain and stimulates your spinal fluid.

- Walk on the grass barefoot for five minutes to take advantage of the earth's magnetic forces. If this isn't possible, at least go for a quick walk outside to pep up your circulation and get your endorphins going.

- Do some dry-skin brushing to energise your whole system.

- Sprinkle some basil and rosemary essential oils on to a tissue and breathe in deeply.

- Play some music of your choice, whatever invigorates you and lifts your mood.

- Spritz yourself with a cold shower for instant energy.

These are just quick, instant energy lifts. For long-term stamina, incorporate the following into your everyday life.

Your Complete Energy Plan

- Make time for yourself every day to switch off and do something that you enjoy.

- Consider your stress levels. Write down anything that makes you feel anxious, and try to decide how you can bring change into your life. Remember, you have the power to choose how **you** run your life.

- Relax and meditate every day for 20 minutes. In the morning, before going to work, is best, to clear your mind so that you can start your day with a positive outlook.

- Check your posture. Keep your breast-bone lifted. Don't tense the muscles at the back of your neck.

- Slow down your breathing.

- Eat a good, whole-food diet.

- Avoid sugar and junk food.

- Don't reduce your calorie intake unless you are seriously overweight. Remember, a calorie is a unit of *energy*.

- If necessary, supplement your diet with a multi-vitamin and mineral tablet.

- Drink plenty of water.

- Think positive! Negativity is the biggest enemy of your energy levels.

- Set harmonising goals in your life so that you can look forward to future events.

- Take regular exercise. Maybe join a yoga class to help your breathing techniques.

- Make sure that you get enough sleep.

- Check your environment. Are you surrounded by electronic equipment where you sleep? Could you be sleeping over an underground stream? Do you need to de-clutter your home or office?

- Think about your spiritual side. Take time out to meditate on the meaning of your life.

- Enjoy sunshine and fresh air whenever you can. Take advantage of Universal Energy and surround yourself with nature whenever you can.

Remember, loss of energy comes about through an imbalance in your life, so to increase your vitality, you need to adjust your lifestyle now. Concentrate on:

- **Healthy Mind**, free of stress, tension and anxiety.

- **Healthy Body**, through regular exercise, slow breathing, good food and plenty of water.

- **Contented Spirit**, through finding time to relax and discover peace within yourself. Try to surround yourself with people who love you or make you happy.

Good luck with your vitality plan! Once you start, you will never look back, and after three months of the above, you will be bouncing with energy!

BIBLIOGRAPHY AND FURTHER READING

Agombar, F., *Beat Fatigue with Yoga*, Element Books/ HarperCollins, 1999/2002

Atkinson, R. et al, *Introduction to Psychology*, Harcourt Brace & Co, 1990

Beck, T. et al, *Cognitive Therapy of Depression*, The Guildford Press, 1979

Coghill, R., *The Book of Magnet Healing*, Gaia Books Ltd., 2000

Collinge, W., *Recovering from M.E.*, Souvenir Press Ltd., 1997

Cowan, D. & Girdlestone, R., *Safe as Houses?*, Gateway Books, 1996

Crawford, M., *Allergies*, Element, 1997

Dillman, E., *The Little Yoga Book*, Time Warner, 1999

Gerber, M.D., *Vibrational Medicine*, Bear & Co., 1996

Gordon, R., *Are you Sleeping in a Safe Place?*, Dulwich Health Society, 1993

Hopkins, C., *Principles of Aromatherapy*, Thorsons, 1996

Jackson, J., *Aromatherapy*, Dorling Kindersley, 1993

Jacobs, G. & Kjaer, J., *Beat Candida through Diet*, Vermilion, 1997

Kelder, P., *Tibetan Secrets of Youth and Vitality*, Thorsons, 1988

Kent, H., *The Complete Illustrated Guide to Yoga*, Element Books, 1999

Levenson, J., *Menace in the Mouth,* Brompton Health, 2000

Ozaniec, N., *The Elements of the Chakras,* Element Books, 1996

Rowley, N., *Basic Clinical Science,* Hodder & Stoughton, 1999

Saraswati, S.S., *Yoga Nidra,* Bihar School of Yoga, 1998

Scrivner, J., *Detox Your Mind,* Piatkus, 1999

Scrivner, J., *Detox Yourself,* Piatkus, 1995

Sears, B., *Enter the Zone,* HarperCollins, 1995

Selby, A., *H_2O,* Collins & Brown, 2000

Sheehan, E., *Low Self-Esteem,* Element Books, 1998

Shomon, M.J., *Living Well with Hypothyroidism,* Avon Books, 2000

Steven, C., *Diabetes,* Element Books, 1995

Stewart, A., *Tired All The Time,* Optima Books, 1993

Teitelbaum, J., *From Fatigued to Fantastic,* Avery, 1999

Thie, J.F., *Touch for Health,* De Vorss & Co., 1979

Too, L., *Feng Shui,* Element Books, 1998

Vaclavek, V., *Magnotherapy – the Phacts (sic),* Corbett & Cavanagh, 1999

Van Straten, M., *The Good Sleep Guide,* Kyle Cathie Ltd, 1993

Articles and Reports:

Agombar, F.J., 'Interview with Stephen Walpol', *Interaction,* Spring 1997

Agombar, F.J., 'Is Medigen the Brainwave needed for ME?', *Interaction,* Autumn 1994

Anthony H.M. et al, 'Effective Allergy Practice', *BSAEM & BSNM,* 1994

Corin, J., 'Cold Water Therapy', *Interaction,* Spring 1995

Diamond N., 'Complementary & Alternative Therapies', *Interaction*, Winter 1998

Downing, D. et al, 'Effective Nutritional Medicine', *BSAEM & BSNM*, 1995

Eaton, K.K. et al, 'Multiple Chemical Sensitivity Recognition & Management', *BSAENM*, 2000

Hipparchia, A., 'ME and Geopathic and Electromagnetic Stress', *Interaction*, Spring 1997

Myers, E., 'Carbon Monoxide Poisoning: Symptoms Identical to ME', *Interaction*, March 2001

Schiernecker, A., 'Treating Like with Like', *Interaction*, August 2000

RESOURCES

Chapter 3: Recharge Your Batteries and Relax Your Body

There are some very good audiotapes around that can be used for relaxation. I particularly recommend tapes from: Lizzie Spring, The Osteopathic and Homeopathic Practice, 4–6 Ashford Road, Tenterden, Kent TN30 6QU. Telephone: 01580 766424. There are four tapes: *Relaxation, Better Health, Turning your Life Around* and *Morning and Evening*. Each tape costs £8.50 which includes postage and packing.

Chapter 4: Relax Your Mind

For Yoga Nidra audiotapes, Angela's Books does an excellent selection. Details from: 65 Norfolk Road, Seven Kings, Ilford, Essex IG3 8LJ. Ken Thompson's *Silent Waters* is particularly good. For more on yoga courses for relaxation contact: The Yoga for Health Foundation, Ickwell Bury, Biggleswade, Bedfordshire SG18 9EF. Telephone 01767 627271 for details of residential courses in the UK. In Australia contact: The Yoga for Health Foundation, PO Box 212, Montville, Queensland 4560; and in South Africa contact: The Yoga for Health Foundation, 4 Barry Road, Pietermaritzburg 3021.

Chapter 11: The *Candida* Connection – Gut Dysbiosis

Clear From Candida is a three-hour video on how to treat *candida* and includes a cookery demonstration. It costs £19.99 which includes a recipe booklet from: Safe Remedies, 144 High Street, Dunbar, East Lothain, EH42 1JJ, telephone 01368 864834.

The National Candida Society, PO Box 151, Orpington, Kent, BR5 1UJ.

This is a national support group offering local group meetings and a quarterly newsletter giving advice on the latest treatments for *candida* and a free telephone helpline. £15 a year membership. Visit their website at: www.candida-society.org.uk.

Chapter 12: Chronic Fatigue Syndrome – Myalgic Encephalopathy

The two main organisations in the UK are: Action for ME, PO Box 1302, Wells, Somerset, BA5 1YE and The ME Association, Stanhope House, High Street, Stanford-le Hope, Essex, SS17 OHA. In South Africa contact: ME Association of South Africa, PO Box 461, Hillcrest 3650, Natal. In Australia contact: Anzymes, PO Box 7, Moonee Ponds, Victoria 3039. Send a self-addressed envelope for details of membership. All these organisations provide a counselling service, fact sheets and membership journals. Action for ME also has details of their support groups nationwide.

Angela Stevens does excellent yoga audiotapes for those with CFS and ME. *Yoga, the Gentle Way* and *Breathe to Live* are particularly good. Angela also trains yoga teachers to run remedial classes for those with CFS/ME. She has a list of teachers across the UK. Write to: Angela Stevens, Laminga, Southview Road, Wadhurst, E. Sussex TN5 6TL for further details. The Yoga For Health Foundation (details above) also runs residential courses for those with ME.

Chapter 14: Diabetes

Diabetes UK, 10 Queen Anne Street, London W1M OBD. Telephone 020 7323 1531. They supply a wide range of fact-sheets on diabetes.

Chapter 16: Mercury in Your Mouth

The British Society for Mercury Free Dentistry, 225 Old Brompton Road, London SW5 OEA. Telephone 020 7736 4145. They can arrange for your fillings to be tested and extracted, if necessary. They also have a list of dentists throughout the UK who specialise in mercury extraction.

There is also a patient support group: Patients against Mercury Amalgam; information line: 020 7256 2994.

Chapter 17: Pollution and Chemical Sensitivities

The British Society for Allergy and Environmental Medicine, PO Box 7, Knighton, LD8 2WF. Telephone 01547 560150. This organisation publishes various leaflets and handbooks, which are very useful for those suffering with chemical problems.

Also visit www.pan-uk.org for up-to-date information on environmental pollution. The Healthy House, Cold Harbour, Ruscombe, Stroud, GL6 6DA, telephone 01453 752216, sells a wide range of environmentally friendly paints and varnishes. Send SAE for their full range.

Chapter 18: Eat Well and Energise

Simply Organic does an excellent range of organic produce, including meat and fish, which is delivered throughout the UK by mail order. Telephone 0845 1000044 or visit www.simplyorganic.net.

Chapter 23 and 24: Basic and Extra Supplements for Energy

Biocare, telephone 0121 433 3727, or Prohealth, (USA) telephone 001-800-366-6056. Both do a good range of all of the supplements mentioned in these chapters. Also, the Nutri Centre 020 7436 5122 does a huge range of supplements. Natural Health Care 01276 678400 has a very helpful pharmacist to give guidance on what to choose for your particular needs and will give you a 15% discount if you mention this book. If you are on the Internet, good sites to visit include: www.immunesupport.com or www.needs.com. Both of these sites are based in the USA but mail-out worldwide. Their supplements are considerably cheaper than UK prices – but you may be charged duty.

Safe Remedies, telephone 013368 864834 does a very good green food called Organic Green Barley powder – excellent for improving energy. Higher Nature, telephone 01435 882880 does a good range of supplements.

Chapter 26: Detox Weekend

Most health food shops and chemists now have long-handled brushes for dry skin brushing. A good cleanser to use during a detox is Eau Thermale by Avene. This is exceptionally high in spa waters and is hypoallergenic.

Avene does a full range of treatment creams – available from Boots and some specialist chemists.

Chapter 31: Touch for Health – And Energy

For the nearest Touch for Health therapist in your area contact: Natalie Davenport, 01453 763035 or Brian Butler, telephone 0208 399 3215.

Chapter 34: Aromatherapy Revivers

Aromatherapy oils are widely available from all good chemists and health food shops. Tisserand and Neal's Yard are particularly good in my opinion. For details of your nearest aromatherapist contact: The International Federation of Aromatherapists, Stamford House, 2–4 Chiswick High Road, London W4.

Chapter 35: Homeopathy for Balance and Harmony

To find a qualified homoeopath in your area contact: The Society of Homeopaths, 4a Artizan Road, Northampton, NN1 4HU, telephone 01604 621400 or visit www.homeopathy-soh.org.

Chapter 36: Electromagnetic Radiation – The Good and the Bad News

Both the Empulse device and the Aegis are available from Natural Health Works, EmDI Ltd, Suffolk Enterprise Centre, Felaw Maltings, 44 Felaw Street, Ipswich, IP2 8SJ. Telephone 01473 407333 or visit www.empulse.com for details of your nearest practitioner. The Empulse costs around £160 and the Aegis about £104. Both come with a money-back guarantee.

The Trimed is currently not being manufactured, but if you have an existing device and would like a new brain scan then contact: Kiti Miranda, The Hale Clinic, 7 Park Crescent, Regent's Park, London W1N 3HE, telephone 020 7631 0604.

The Coghill Field Mouse, a hand-held device which measures how strong EMFs are, is available from: Electro-magnetic Products, Alexander House, Pontypool, Gwent, NP4 5UH, telephone 01495 752122. The device costs around £99 plus VAT.

Chapter 37: Magnet Therapy

A wide range of therapeutic magnets is available from: Jackie Cary-Elwes, Magnets for Health, Poplar Hall, The Street, Appledore, Kent TN24 2AF, telephone 01233 758334. They can recommend which type and strength is right for your particular condition. Also, Electro-magnetic Products, as above, also supply magnets.

Chapter 38: Geopathic Stress

Alf Riggs, 33 Parvills, Parkland Estate, Waltham, Essex, EN9 1QG, telephone 01992 719735. Mr Riggs, as mentioned in the text, is a well-known dowser. Also, Environmental Harmony, Walpole Hatch Farm, Halesworth, Suffolk, IP19 9BB, telephone 01986 784700 can advise on treatment for geopathic stress and will visit anywhere in the UK. They can also dowse and diagnose from a distance.

Chapter 40: Energise your Environment with Feng Shui

If you would like your house of office seen by a feng shui expert the following organisations can recommend a practitioner in your area:
Feng Shui Association, telephone 02273 69384, Feng Shui Network International, telephone 020 7935 8935, Feng Shui Society, telephone 020 8567 2043.

Chapter 45: Sunshine, the Energy Generator

For more information on Seasonal Affective Disorders send an SAE to: SAD Association, PO Box 989, London SW7 2PX. For a range of full-spectrum light boxes contact: SAD Lightbox Co. Ltd, Unit 48, Marlowe Road, Stokenchurch, High Wycombe, Bucks, HP14 3QJ. Telephone: 01494 484 851. 2,500 lux is the minimum needed to treat SAD. Lightboxes start from £93.50 – and I would recommend using a box of 10,000 lux. Higher Nature, Burwash Common, E Sussex TN19 7BR have just started to sell a range of full-spectrum lights. They are considerably cheaper than the boxes as they can be used as light bulbs around the home and cost about £24.00 Higher Nature claims that you can get as much benefit from working with their lights, as by using a 3,000 lux box. Telephone 01435 882880 for more details.

Index

Note: page numbers in *italics* refer to illustrations.